Mourning and Dancing
for Schools

Mourning and Dancing for Schools

A Grief and Recovery Sourcebook for Students, Teachers and Parents

Sally Downham Miller, Ph.D.

Health Communications, Inc.
Deerfield Beach, Florida

www.hci-online.com
www.kidsgrieve.org

We would like to acknowledge the following individuals who granted us permission to reprint the cited material.

Emily's Eulogy, by Cynthia Rice. Reprinted with permission of the author.

Jason Remembers His Friend Mandy, by Jason Wilson. Reprinted with permission of the author.

Cory Remembers His Friend Joby, by Cory Malchow. Reprinted with permission of the author.

Mandy Remembers Her Friend Amity, by Amanda Jackson. Reprinted with permission of Carol Jackson.

Library of Congress Cataloging-in-Publication Data

Miller, Sally Downham.
    Mourning and dancing for schools : a grief and recovery
sourcebook for students, teachers, and parents /
Sally Downham Miller.
    p.   cm.
    ISBN 1-55874-775-3 (trade paper)
    1. School crisis management—United States.
    2. Counseling in education—United States.   3. Grief.
    I. Title.
    LB2866.5 .M54 2000
    371.4'6—dc21

                                 00-040924

Publisher: Health Communications, Inc.
             3201 S.W. 15th Street
             Deerfield Beach, FL 33442-8190

Cover illustrations by Lisa Camp
Inside book design by Dawn Grove

In memory of

Carolyn Sue Small

and

in honor of

the Traphagen School family

Contents

Preface

I have been in education for twenty-five years and have taught everything from kindergarten to college. During those years, few of my constituents knew that at the age of twenty-four, I became a widow and an employed, single parent of two preschool children. The day my husband died, my life changed forever, but I didn't talk about it at school. I didn't talk about it with anyone. I knew nothing about other people's grief, except what television showed us of famous people's funerals. I remember how I felt when John F. Kennedy was shot. So, when Bob died I tried to emulate the grieving behavior of JFK's wife, Jacqueline, and then Coretta Scott King and Ethel Kennedy. The only problem was there was no television coverage of the weeks, months and years after the funerals. I was left in the dark. No one talked about it.

I eventually went back to college and became a teacher. My children grew up and went to school. School became our major family focus. No one spoke about grief there either. In the late 1970s, I began spending time with people who were struggling with their grief, not because I had any answers, but because I knew what it is like to go through it alone. I learned that "being there" with people who are grieving is helpful. They don't feel so alone. I talked to them. They talked to me. Together we helped each other. We encouraged each other to keep doing what each of us had to do alone. Whenever someone called me, I found time to go. All of my contacts with individuals, families, hospice groups, churches and other agencies came over the years by word of mouth.

In the early 1980s, I went into school administration, all the while continuing to work with people who were grieving. I started my first support group and people came. I never advertised. I was not paid for this work. I did not put it on my resume. I felt certain that what I was doing was not according to directives of the National Institute of Mental Health or research in the area of psychology. Perhaps that was because, in the general public, no one was talking about grief work. One Friday night I spoke at a school in Paterson, New Jersey, and some people were there from a church where I had spoken the month before. I asked them why they had come, and one of them said, "Because you are the only game in town." They became my groupies and were eventually my best critics. After attending my speeches, they would go out for coffee and tell their own stories and critique my session. Through the years, I learned from all of these wonderful individuals how much we need each other and what helps in the grieving experience. And a new philosophy began to form.

I became a school principal in 1985. Like most others, my school was carefully organized and tightly structured, and every activity of a student's day was scheduled right down to the minute. Most staff members have little information, less time and uneven knowledge on handling grief at school. One child might lose a parent and have a teacher who manages to make time for encouraging discussions that provide direction and confidence for going on. Another student might encounter someone who believes in old cliches, like "Why would you bring that up here?" "Talking about it won't change anything," "This discussion should take place at home," "You should be over that by now" and "Why would you dig all of that back up again?" As a school principal I began working closely with families. Students died. Teachers lost children. Students lost pets and grandparents. To my dismay, I found they were not given much time to deal with their grief.

Yet, we who are parents, teachers and school administrators can all tell stories about students and families who have never recovered from losses. We have watched our children helplessly while their interest in school declines and their grades go down. We watch them hang out with the wrong crowd and begin medicating themselves. We are appalled at the rate of adolescent depression, suicide and drug use that is reaching down to our elementary schools. Still, we are hesitant to speak about the overwhelming, powerful, life-changing effects of loss and grief.

Twenty-five years of working with grieving families, schools and individuals have proven to me that there are some things that work: acknowledging grief instead of pretending it is not there, accepting the reality that grieving is a painful but natural part of life, being with people who are experiencing it, and talking with people about what helps. This isn't rocket science. It isn't against the law. It isn't easy, but it is simple. It can be done in schools. It can save lives.

Acknowledgments

A side from my family members, who are my lifeline, many friends and colleagues have helped me with various parts of this book: reading, editing, researching, listening, and giving me their honest input and feedback. All of them — teachers, administrators, child advocates, school counselors, parents and therapists — wanted to assist in making this book helpful to its readers. My friends and colleagues who generously gave of their time, insight and wisdom include: Jane Boswell, Eileen Cederberg, Joe Heath, Brenda Kirleis, Bill Lindbloom, Jenny Murtaugh, Nancy Nargi, Sue Naumann, John Murgia, Louise Potterton, Suzy Scott, Brenda Spencer, Jack Szabo, Linda and Don Waters, and Dave Wright. I am especially grateful to Marian Brovero for the hours spent researching books and resources for children and for always being focused on issues of the heart. I also wish to thank my friend and literary agent, Linda Roghaar, and my niece, Laura Downham Pytko, for her leadership in starting the Rainbows program in Waldwick. My husband, Will Miller, endured my fits of writing, handled technical problems, fixed tea and willingly loved the author through this book's completion. He also took charge of development of *www.kidsgrieve.org,* the Web site that will extend the work of this book to schools and parents across the country. The editorial gifts of Matthew Diener, Lisa Drucker, Erica Orloff and Susan Tobias sewed this book together and made it "fit to print." I wish also to thank all of the good people at HCI, who have shared my vision for grief work in schools, and who generously ignored my deadlines and supported my efforts at Traphagen School.

Those to whom I am most grateful are the families in this book. I am honored that they would allow me to include the stories of their lives and loved ones. I salute you from my heart:

The Camp Tecumseh Family
The Dick Family
The Downham Family
The Foschini Family
The Greene Family
The Jackson Family
The Landis Family
The Major Family
The Murgia Family
The Naumann Family
The Rice Family
The Skehan Family
The Small Family
The Traphagen School Family
The Waldwick Educational Community

Introduction

Crisis management teams have become adept at handling trauma in our schools. They heed the call. They know the drill. They perform emotional and psychological triage in the aftermath of death and other traumatic events. The interventions of these counselors and the teams they assemble are lifesaving. They help scabs form over painful wounds. The deep healing, however, does not take place in the first few days or even the first few weeks. This is not news to any of us. We know that the imprints left by loss and trauma, especially in a child's life, are there long after order is restored and the ceremonies have ended. That is when the work of grieving and healing begins. For, as surely as the sun comes up, children will continue to experience the effects of their losses for years to come, some of them for their lifetime. The topic of "helping people grieve over time," however, does not get the same attention as "dealing with death and crisis and the immediate aftermath." It doesn't have the same pizzazz. It doesn't grab the public eye. Crisis management work makes headlines. The longer, painstaking, time-consuming work of processing grief does not generate much press coverage.

Mourning and Dancing for Schools is about the less publicized grief work in schools, grades kindergarten through twelve. It is about interventions that help students in the school family a week later, four months later, years later. It is about understanding the reality that some life-changing losses can affect us for the rest of our lives, but that does not mean we are doomed to suffer in silence or live out a diminished existence.

This is a book about hope. It is about finding ways to deal with the deep, passion-filled experiences we know as grief. It is about understanding the ways young people act out their feelings, be they repressed or expressed in eruptive fits. It is about recognizing the changes that occur as a result of loss, acknowledging the effects of these changes and learning how to manage them. It proposes training, interventions and ongoing work of a Grief and Loss Team that can help restore health and healing after the counselors brought in during a crisis go back to their own jobs. It is not a replacement program for school counselors, nor is it a grief therapy program. It is not a curriculum for teaching death education, nor is it a book about preventing violence or crises in our schools. Inherent in this philosophy, however, is the belief that helping children find ways to live with loss and to work through grief and giving them hope can reduce some of the tragedies that occur in our school families.

Violence is often described as an explosion of powerful, pent-up, misunderstood emotions. Unresolved grief is often described as a suppression of powerful, pent-up, difficult-to-understand emotions resulting from a death or tragedy or trauma. So, a by-product of this work could be a clearer understanding of deep emotional reactions and the reduction and redirection of the violent impulse. This is a training manual for people who want to work with students who are grieving in our school communities, and this can include teachers, administrators, students, counselors and parents, because all of us want to do something, but no one wants to do the wrong thing. So usually very little is done.

This new approach to grief and loss is similar to the approach we have taken with other former taboos like AIDS and other sexually transmitted diseases, harassment and abuse, drug and alcohol addictions. We know this is a healthy approach, because it follows other healthy models like physical therapy, rehabilitation, recovery programs for addictions and most religious tenets for working through the pain and misery of life.

Even though this work may meet up with some resistance by people inside and outside of the schools, most agree that it is important and needed. It begins with having an open dialog about what grief is, how it affects our students at different developmental stages, and what strategies work for dealing with grief that can be employed by teachers, parents and anyone working with kids. It is not complicated, but it does require a new way of thinking about this subject and learning what to say and do.

The pages that follow are a combination of true-life stories in schools and information about helping schools. Like grieving and healing, these two dimensions interact to offer a new approach to helping students and their families learn to live with life's losses. The stories are offered as learning opportunities for the readers and teams. The lessons and resources are to be considered templates for creating a program specifically for your school or community. (Refer to *www.kidsgrieve.org.*) It can be an active, expanding program that extends beyond the school proper or as simple as information-sharing for future needs.

The first story is the most extensive of the book, as it gives a day-by-day, week-to-week account of an extraordinary and unwelcome experience I had working with a school whose teachers, students and parents were grieving.

Part I

A School in Grief

Carolyn: A School Principal

DAY ONE

I stood in front of her chair and ran my fingers along the beveled edges of her desk, not ready to sit down, unable to take my eyes off of her "to do" list. That familiar handwriting spelled out her activities for today. The items with "1's" next to them in the left margins were the things she would be doing now. Students were in their classes, teachers were teaching, the secretary was filling out the morning reports and I was there staring at her notes. Her perfume was traceable as the morning breeze moved the air in the office. Her pumpkin sweater hung on the back of her door. The teddy bears she kept to reach and motivate her students sat silently holding their signs, advertising the character values she doggedly pursued: responsibility, caring, honesty.

I turned her nameplate around to face me. It did not say "Carolyn Small, Principal." It said, "Carolyn Small, Head

Learner." I could hear her voice in my weary mind. Surely, I thought, she will come blowing through the door any minute now, shouting greetings, asking questions, pulling one of the scarves she always wore from around her neck, hanging up her coat, putting on one of her child/holiday-oriented sweaters. "Hey, Babes," she would surely say, "what are we learning today?" In all of my years of school administration, no colleague had ever called me, "Babes." She was one of a kind, a dynamo, a champion of kids. And now she was dead. In a flash, almost as she lived, her light went out from this world in a moment, in a highway accident from which everyone else walked away. It was not her fault.

We had been elementary school principals together in a small, northern New Jersey school system called Waldwick. I left the year before to pursue a writing career, and she had come to visit our home in Indiana the previous month, the week before school started. She knew I was closing in on the deadline for this book, so she offered to help. *Help?* I thought. *How could she help?* But she did. I asked her about her experience handling death in her schools, and she began telling me two accounts of student deaths, for which she carefully nurtured a grieving/memorial process. Her stories were so vivid and poignant; I stopped her and ran for a tape recorder. Now I have her voice on tape talking about death and grief and what she thought was important and healthy in handling them.

I was on a book tour when the accident happened. My husband reached me in the city where I was speaking and gave me the unbelievable news. I returned home in shock to find fifteen messages waiting for me, from the superintendent, other administrators, teachers and friends, telling me of her untimely death. But the first message was from Carolyn. "Hey, Will and Sally, it's the Smalls here. You can run from us but you can't hide. It's October, and you promised us a visit. I'm cooking you guys a big Italian meal, and I want to know when you are coming East. I'll be at home tonight. We're going to a wedding tomorrow, and we'll be home on Sunday. Call me. I can't wait to see you. I have the pasta water on."

Upon hearing her voice I had laid down on the bed and cried. How could all of that be gone?

Now, I was at her school. I wanted to be there when teachers and students arrived. I wanted to hug every person who was as bewildered as I. I wanted to be a part of this horrible, powerful experience. I certainly did not want to be alone. Grief from a distance seems less real, so it is easier to pretend it is not so. And that only postpones the flood of emotions that seem to intensify with time if left unaddressed. So I came. The superintendent had asked in one of our conversations if I would take over running the school. I said, "Of course." The teachers who hugged me asked if I would "help them through this." I said, "Of course." Parents asked me if I would help their children, and I wondered as I said, "Of course," what I could find inside of my grieving self that could possibly help anyone. I didn't think that a grief expert who is grieving is worth much. To which I silently said, "Of course." But I came anyway, because that is what all of us can always do, regardless of how we are feeling.

Grief takes place over time, but it doesn't take place all the time. It includes a powerful, sometimes overwhelming, combination of reactions to the loss that has occurred. It takes our brains time to adjust to this phenomenon, but the process begins almost immediately, even in the periods of

shock and denial. It does take time, though, and the question everyone wants answered is "How long?" To complicate answering that query, we all know that the heart takes
a little longer to adjust to what the mind knows. So we can
see that the answers vary widely and seldom can be measured in days or years or stages. We also have a society with
expectations, real or assumed, for people who are grieving
that are reported by many as out-of-sync with the experience. Our quick-fix, follow-these-steps culture televises
people grieving in the immediate aftermath of a tragedy or
death and determines to help them find healing and closure
during the first days or week of their grief. The conversations on the subject seem to imply a period of grieving and
a period of healing, as though they are mutually exclusive.

As Carolyn's story will demonstrate, the "time to mourn
and time to dance" cannot be as easily measured and separated, as it can be allowed. It recognizes that grief and healing are interactive in our lives and that "mourning and
dancing" are strands of the same cord or lifeline that weaves
through all of our lives. It promotes the philosophy that it is
healthy to mourn when the response or emotion is experienced, either alone or with others. Permission to do so is
hereby given. If other voices in our society, including our
own, refuse to grant permission, don't listen. Refusals to
discuss grief usually arise out of our own unprocessed grief.
As this book will discuss, such a refusal is likely an invalid
voice of guilt or fear, not wise counsel. This philosophy for
incorporating grief in our lives asserts that this work takes
time, primarily allowing the time for it when the occasion
arises, if not in the moment, then shortly thereafter. This
often requires having a way to deal with it, in order to bring
it outside of ourselves. That "way" usually includes someone

else, with whom it can be processed in a safe and supportive place. It is not comfortable, "feel good" stuff, but it can bring comfort and help others gain strength and feel a little better. And isn't that the goal here, to have the strength to go on and to feel better? When we feel good we usually do good things for others and ourselves.

DAY TWO: MEETING WITH THE TEACHERS

The teachers walked into the All-Purpose Room in the same silent reverence in which people enter church. The crisis management team had done a fantastic job of preparing for the day. There was a handout for the staff that included information about how children understand death at various developmental stages, common misinformation about death that abounds in our culture, ideas about talking with children, options for answering difficult questions in class, etc. They also had delicious rolls, coffee cake and bagels. Hot coffee with real cream was served on a table with candles burning next to a bouquet of fall flowers. All of this said, "We care; we are in this together; we want to give you all the support you need to get through this day." There were boxes of tissues everywhere. Never underestimate the nurturing effects of easy-to-digest food, hot soups or beverages, and extra touches that convey caring and warmth and understanding.

When the superintendent turned the meeting over to me I felt anew the impotence we all feel when facing death and those "left behind." I began in a voice that seemed incapable of much volume and told them I was honored to be there on Carolyn's behalf, and most importantly to be with them. I reminded them of my own grief that certainly trumped the part of me that was a grief expert. I spoke of the mystifying qualities of shock and denial, the disorientation, the inability to focus, the nonexistent attention span that led me in distracted circles, going from one project to the next without finishing any. I welled up with tears and reminded them of the healing effects of crying, that it stimulates our immune system and releases endorphins from our brains. I also gave them the tip about Kleenex: Have tissues available at arm's length from someone who is crying, but don't hand them a tissue, because that very gesture says, "Stop crying, blow your nose and dry your tears." I encouraged them to allow themselves to grieve when the urge came. They may be the only example these children would have to model.

At one point in this meeting, a teacher asked me an excellent question. In my attempt to answer, my mind got distracted and I couldn't remember what we were talking about. Fortunately, Janet, one of our school social workers, could "see" what was happening. She gently interrupted and said, "Another suggestion for answering that question is. . . ." I thanked her for being there when my thought processes shut down, and pointed out that I demonstrated a perfect example of how grief works. Janet's attentiveness and skill felt supportive, her understanding comforting. I was reminded of how good it feels to be part of a team and to have someone "take my part" when I drop the ball.

We talked about the way children grieve in spurts. Crying then playing. Staring then laughing. Irritated for no reason then caught up in delight. I also talked about the comfort of routine. Grief requires so much of our attention, because it takes energy to think in new ways, interact in new ways and trust in new ways. We long for distraction, peace, sleep. We want to go to bed and wake up and have things as they were yesterday, when we knew what to expect, what to count on, what to do. So I suggested that these teachers plan their day in spurts. A little teaching, a grief activity, read a book, go for a walk. I encouraged them to follow the daily schedule as much as possible, because it is reassuring to look at the clock and to know that at 9:30 we have gym and then to go to the gym. So many other things have changed.

I told them how unfair it was that we who are grieving have the added task of teaching others about grief, even when we are not teachers. So it was twice as difficult for them because they were there that day as teachers, soon to have their students in front of them, trying to focus and make sense and teach. I offered to go into any class that wanted me to come and talk about death or Mrs. Small or to read *The Fall of Freddie the Leaf* or to answer questions or to give them a break. I went to a number of classes, but not one teacher took a break. Dedicated, caring teachers are like that. The district had arranged counselors at every grade level, in every building and in the library for any student or teacher who wanted to talk. I offered to have children come to the principal's office, when I was not in a class. There the students could see that things were still the same in her office and that the school was still running from that hub.

As a schoolwide activity, we decided to use the character tree, painted on the wall in the All-Purpose Room, as a symbol of Mrs. Small's life. We thought students could write or draw messages on construction-paper leaves to express their sadness or appreciation. Rik, the art teacher, offered to have students make the leaves for the whole school in art classes that day. This would accomplish two goals: the

production of creative tools for expressing grief and a caring activity that art classes could give to the other students.
We all seemed to need to "do" something. When there is a
sudden death there is no chance to say "good-bye" or "thank
you for helping" or "I liked your sweater" or "I miss you."
When the students would enter the All-Purpose Room in
the coming weeks for lunch or gym class or an assembly,
they would know their messages were on her tree. I read the
leaves later in the day. One of them said,

Dear Mrs. Small,

Please visit my Grandmother when you get to Heaven, she is
already there. I love you both very much.

                                                    Sara

I did not tell the teachers at the end of our meeting that
their students would remember this day for the rest of their
lives. They already had enough pressure.

Following my meeting with the teachers, I stood outside
greeting students as they arrived for school. I introduced
myself as the principal from the other school. I told them
that I had come to be with them and to help their school,
because we all miss Mrs. Small so much. Parents cried, and
children looked mostly bewildered. Some, who would not
have otherwise done so, held hands and patted each other
on the shoulder and carried each other's things. When all of
the children were in class, I turned on the intercom and
asked everyone to join me in a moment of silence.

In the book *Refrigerator Rights,* a premise is put forth that
applies to the grief work we needed to do in Carolyn's
school. It proposes that we have become so geographically

dispersed, so isolated in our personal lives, that we have lost our extended families, longtime neighbors and lifetime friends. These are the individuals with whom we used to talk around the kitchen table about politics, religions, life, death and people. These relationships and interactions provided a vehicle for examining life's remedies and a proving ground to test "what works." It was a group with whom we did not always agree but with whom we felt safe. These were, mostly, people who cared about us but did not necessarily have to live with us. The levels of honesty and challenge encouraged us to think about what we were doing with our lives, instead of watching others live out made-up lives on television.

It is difficult to handle loss and the resulting grief alone. It cannot be processed only in the mind, by thinking our way through it. So how can we build into our lives a group of people to support us through this hard work? It is not likely that we will be moving back to our old neighborhood, where Grandma and Uncle Mike and old Mrs. Smith and our cousins all got together on Sundays for a big meal and talked around the table or went for a walk. It takes time to develop the kind of relationships where we can go into someone else's home and open the refrigerator and get something to drink and sit down at the table and unload. Instead, we have moved away to pursue the American Dream. We are so busy pursuing the dream, making ends meet, working, caring for our homes and growing our families that we rely on the impersonal and isolated conveniences of the television or the Internet for company or "contact."

The good news is that there are some forms of the extended family and old neighborhood around in our lives today, like churches, community organizations and, the focus of this book, our community schools. There we find stability in the family-like structure. The mature, experienced staff works with the growing student population in a safe, challenging environment. The goal is the successful education, learning and development of the students. Like the old neighborhood and our extended families we don't always agree with each other or like everyone, but we respect the right of each to be a part of the group, working toward the same goal. By its very makeup, the school family is a healthy place for a person who is grieving to find remedies, advice and support, if we can just get over the social taboo of not talking about it.

In the not-too-distant past, grief was not discussed at school. We have heard stories about when a child died and his or her desk was removed and that child's name was not spoken . . . out of respect for the dead, of course. If there were any questions raised or emotions expressed by students, they were directed to "discuss it at home." Subject closed. Today, thankfully, we have moved beyond that philosophy. Now, crisis management teams formulate plans and handle each crisis as it occurs. There is information available to assist in this endeavor, like Louise Aldrich's *Sudden Death: Crisis in the School*, and school counseling personnel have learned how to tap into their community's helping profession's agencies and staff. Counselors are brought into the school to provide supportive intervention where needed. The success of this effort depends on the careful planning and orchestration of the team, and by the time the ceremonies are over their work is done. Then the people on the crisis management team, who have other jobs, return to them, hopefully with a sense of accomplishment. One of the important things we have learned from the crisis management model is that students and teachers alike appreciate having all of those counselors around. They report that knowing they are "there" helps, even if there is no interaction. They report feeling supported, reinforced, and everyone is grateful for their presence. But then what?

DAY TWO: MIDMORNING

Word had been sent out via the class phone chain that parents were encouraged to come together as a school family as soon as their children were in their classes. So parents gathered in the All-Purpose Room. The moms and dads of the Parent School Organization had made fresh coffee, and I went in there to share with these shocked and saddened people the facts about the accident. They wanted to know. We all want to know. It is in the asking and the retelling of what happened that we strive to "make sense" out of the senseless. This is a helpful process for all of us, because we have to reprogram our brains, and going over the information again and again helps us do that. It isn't morbid; it is necessary. It isn't disrespectful; it is helpful.

Together we discussed answering the tough questions students may ask. For instance, if Mrs. Small was thrown from the car in the accident, does that mean she did not have on her seat belt? Their desire to say the right thing to their children was written on their faces. At an administrative meeting the day before, a member of the crisis management team posed the same question, and we wrestled with the answer. The wisdom that prevailed was that none of us knew what happened, because we were not there. We discussed a number of possible answers, like the seat belt malfunctioned or it was not fitted in the buckle correctly, but in reality, none of us knew for sure. What we did know is what we could talk about and that was this: Mrs. Small always wore her seat belt. Anyone who ever rode in her car knew that, and if her passengers did not have on their belts, she would tell them to buckle up. She always wanted to do the safe and right thing, and all who knew her knew that was the truth. So we focused on what we knew and discussed the simplest way to tell that to the children. With the help of the team members, I told them about the importance of honesty. It was one of the target character values that year at the school, so the students were primed for honesty. I suggested that we talk about Mrs. Small's death as exactly that: She died; she did not "pass away." Passing away is a familiar social euphemism for adults, but it is not a part of children's daily language. They talk about pets dying, leaves dying, goldfish dying. Passing has more to do with moving from class to class or grade to grade, getting a good grade, and having a slip of paper that allows them to go to the nurse's office.

I encouraged these parents to talk with their children about the realities of death and, in particular, the physical realities, like when people die, their body no longer can hear or feel anything and their spirit is gone from their bodies. I related true stories about primary-grade students in other places who had taken food and blankets to the cemetery, because they did not understand. I told the parents that as a public school we couldn't address the spiritual beliefs of various families, so this was their job. They were the only ones who could talk best about their family beliefs and religious theology as it relates to God and eternal life and "going to heaven."

We also discussed the natural fears all of this would bring

up with children. It is a natural sequence to go from "if my principal died" to "then my mom might die." We encouraged again honesty and simplicity. We cannot promise that no one will die, but we can discuss the facts, like accidents rarely happen and are not "the way things are supposed to be." We mostly needed to reassure the children of their safety and the safety of their loved ones. Reassuring comments, about everyone working together to be extra cautious and safe, are helpful. If a child asks point blank, "You aren't going to die, are you, Daddy?" we need to have an answer planned. One idea is to say, "I'll bet I am going to live to be an old man with grandchildren, and those will be your children. I wonder what you will say to them." It is important to remove the fear of impending death away from them, so they have the freedom to "talk about" the current situation in a safe, reassuring setting.

Next, I told the parents that I gave them permission to cry. I repeated the biological facts about crying and the way our bodies are strengthened when we do so. I reminded them that while few of us like to cry, the relief from having cried feels good. Even more so than with the teachers, I encouraged them to let their children see them cry and show them the honesty of sadness following a loss. Grief is about pain, and children need to learn about it. I told them that expressions of grief that do not completely overwhelm the individual are a healthy model for their children. To hide tears or apologize for them says there is something wrong with grief, and great grief is a normal response to great love or respect. The urge to spare our children from pain hinders their growth. It gives them a message that they should pretend not to be in pain, rather than to learn healthy ways to deal with it.

I told them about two children's books that might be

helpful. One is *There's No Such Thing as a Dragon* by Jack Kent. In this fable, a little boy awakens one day to find a tiny dragon on the foot of his bed. He is so excited that he runs downstairs to tell his mother, who predictably says, "You know there is no such thing as a dragon." Then when the child goes back upstairs he finds that the dragon has grown a little bigger. And the entire book is a sequence of the child telling someone about the dragon, which draws the same response, until the dragon is so big its head is out the front door, tail out the back. It is only when the mail carrier remarks to the father about how big their dragon has grown that they acknowledge the dragon's existence. At that point, the dragon begins to shrink. The lesson is clear that in a child's mind, and even in adult thinking, trying to deny what "is" takes up more space and energy and thought than if we just admitted its existence. The poem by Terry Kettering, "There Is an Elephant in My Living Room," has the same message.

The book *The Tenth Good Thing About Barney* by Judith Viorst provides a wonderful exercise that parents could use to engage their children in a nonthreatening activity to process grief. In this book, a family has lost its pet bird, and everyone is sad. The reminders of what the pet did and the role it held in the family were not discussed because they made everyone cry. Finally, someone suggested they talk about all of the good things about Barney, and they began making a list. They did not stop until they had ten. This is a great exercise because everyone can name the three or four outstanding qualities of a person, but it is when you get to six and seven and eight that you list the "little" or "everyday" qualities that are so important.

I told the parents about the exercises I was going to do in

the classrooms with the students in the coming days and weeks that were similar to those just mentioned. Using Leo Buscaglia's *The Fall of Freddie the Leaf*, which is a beautiful metaphor for life and death, I would stimulate conversation about what Mrs. Small taught them. Then I would make the leap from "here is what you learned" to "now you can teach this to someone else," and in so doing keep a part of Mrs. Small with them for the rest of their lives. Then I told them about the egg analogy I share with students, which I used with my own daughter when she asked me, "Where did Daddy go when he died?"

I went to the kitchen and called Tamara in. Sitting her up on the cabinet I said I had a story to tell and pulled an egg from the refrigerator. I asked her what it was, what the insides were called, what part we eat, and how we get the good part out. She loved easy quizzes and answered as though we were playing school. Then I asked, "What do we do with the shell after we have eaten the good part?" "Throw it out," she replied with smug confidence of sure success at the game. "Right," I smiled, "because we don't need it anymore. Its job was to protect all of the good stuff inside, until it was time for it to come out." "Right," she affirmed.

I put my arms around her and snuggled her real close. Then I told her that we were kind of like that egg. We have a shell and that's what we see and feel: our skin, our bones, our eyes and hair. But the good part of us we can't see. That's the part of us that loves each other, that hurts when we see a lost puppy, or wants to help out when we see someone hurt or sick. It's the part of her that wants to make me feel better when I'm crying and wants to feed the ducks at the park when it is cold and windy in the winter. She seemed to be following my line, so I went on, even a little uncertain myself where we were going with this. "And that's the part of us God loves and wants to take to heaven to live with him when we die. Then we don't need these old shells anymore." Her eyes were widening when she asked, "So do we just throw them away?" "Well, not exactly," I continued. "Since we are more valuable to each other than eggshells, we put our body-shells in a box called a casket. It's kind of like a jewelry box, and we bury it in a special place in the ground."

Later that evening we stood by Bob's grave. She put some flowers she had picked in a little can on the stone. I watched her hair blow in the last rays of the setting sun. The gentle look of understanding on her face made her seem many years older than the five young years she possessed.

(From *Mourning & Dancing*)

Before the session ended, parents asked questions, which I answered with the help of the Crisis Management Team. The team could see my exhaustion and interjected caring and practical answers. I used myself again as a perfect example of how disoriented we become when we are first hit with a grievous loss. I reminded them that as they had lost a principal, I had lost a dear friend and colleague. I, too, was grieving. But in my grief and my desire to go crawl under a blanket, I knew that our connection to each other was the most lasting comfort we could receive. So, we sipped coffee and hugged each other and sat close. Just like a family should do.

Through these interactions we were building a philosophy, an attitude, a posture for handling grief. That philosophy endorses an approach for processing the powerful experience of grief by beginning with our own losses, even though different from the present situation, or seemingly less important than the present event. They are the source of empathy. This approach also is rooted in the belief that we are stronger when we are working together—feeling attached, not separated. Being part of a team of coworkers, parents, classmates and colleagues brings insight, strength and comfort. Attachment facilitates the will to live, when loss has made us feel like giving up and dying. It's where healing begins. Each of the practical lessons in this book exemplifies this philosophy. I did not want to be at Carolyn Small's funeral or in her school after her death, but I knew it was the right thing and the healthiest thing I could do.

After the parent meeting, I went into Carolyn's office and tried again to sit at her desk and do some work. There were purchase orders to sign, field trips to approve and memos to write. Mechanically I plodded through the tasks, thankful for a brief time to be dealing with paper and pencils. Then someone would come in or a memory would flood over me, and I wondered if I could get through the day. Sometimes it helps to keep the long view limited to five minutes or the "next task." To look farther down the road can be overwhelming. I was thankful I was going to be there awhile, because I have learned that grief takes place over time, but not all of the time. Small doses help.

END OF DAY TWO

That afternoon and evening, I went to the funeral home. By the time I arrived, the line circled out the door and many families were standing on line with their children. So I tried to make contact with them, in particular to talk to the children, reminding them of what we had mentioned earlier in the day:

that this was just her body and now we need to remember all
the things we loved about her while she was with us. One little
boy said to his mother as he came out of the funeral home that
he knew what I meant. It seemed evident to him that Mrs.
Small's "sparkle" is what had gone on to heaven. I thought
that was a pretty good description of it all.

DAY THREE

The funeral mass was held in a huge church that seemed
cavernous and impossible to fill, but it was standing room
only. One of the priests, Father Dowd, caught my eye and
nodded. He knew I was speaking in the service and that it
would be hard for me. The last time he and Carolyn and I
were together we were in ridiculous outfits playing in the
town's charity basketball game against the Harlem Wizards.
I remembered saying to him that I felt like a fool, when
Carolyn interrupted and said, "Fools! Are you crazy? This
is wonderful. We'll be great!" I marveled at her attitude. It
seemed to work then, and I wondered if it would work now.
I could almost hear her saying to me regarding her own
eulogy, "Are you crazy? Don't worry! You'll be great!"
Then when all of the teachers and our friends came in and
sat around me I began to believe her words, even though my
stomach was in knots.

I was happy that my legs carried me up the altar steps to
the podium. I remembered that my husband reminded me
not to whisper when I spoke, because no one could hear me.
It struck me funny, this idea that I might not be heard, I
who could be heard in a lunchroom with three hundred
children. Most people heard me before they saw me. But
Will knows me and knows that when emotion creeps up my

throat, I whisper. And today I wanted to be heard. I wanted to bring honor to a colleague's memory. I wanted to paint once again a word picture of this dear, charismatic friend. So I swallowed and prayed for my clearest voice.

"I bring greetings and deepest sympathy from the educational community, from the part of Carolyn's life that had occupied her career affections since the age of seventeen when she said, 'I'm going to be a teacher.' In honor of her life and service, the Waldwick Public Schools are closed for the day. The last time the Board of Education closed the schools was for a hurricane called Floyd. Today they have closed them for a whirlwind called Carolyn."

The congregation began to chuckle as soon as I mentioned Hurricane Floyd. They knew the analogy I was going to draw even before I said it. They knew, because they knew Carolyn. And that is what everyone wanted on this day: a little piece of Carolyn. To remember, to retouch and to reconnect with that which felt so ephemeral and unreachable. Words alone cannot do that. We need symbols, ceremony, ritual and remembrance that reach a depth that words cannot plunge.

END OF WEEK ONE

The school librarian, Marge, and I were sitting in Carolyn's office discussing a scheduling problem, when over her shoulder I saw a white-haired man, who looked somewhat familiar, talking to the secretary. I heard her say to him that I would be free shortly, and I wondered if I should know him. I said to Marge, "Do a favor for me and stand up and look in the outer office at that guy with white hair and see if you know him. He looks familiar, but I can't figure out who he is."

She did as I asked and turned around and said, "Oh, Sally, that's Bob Foschini; you remember him. He taught sixth grade here until he retired a few years ago." Instantly, I remembered, but the image had changed drastically. The guy I remembered was a robust, energetic person with a fun-loving personality. This person was a stoop-shouldered, depressed-looking person with red-rimmed eyes. He looked like he had been crying. I asked Marge if he knew Carolyn, and she said, "I don't think so." I looked back again, and he had moved out of my line of sight. Marge continued, "He lost a son this summer."

"A son! What happened?" I asked. She wasn't sure, but thought it was something like leukemia. Then she told me that Bob and his wife, Rosemary, had kept him in their home when nothing more could be done, and he died with his family around him. *What a gift*, I thought. But that gift comes with a price and that price often includes wondering if you did the right thing. Blaming yourself for being alive. Feeling parent-guilt, irrationally, for not succeeding in saving his life. And after the funeral, the home, where all of your energy and focus was on the medical/hospice effort, seems devoid of meaning and purpose.

I finished my meeting with Marge and walked out to open my arms to this aching father. I felt his stomach constrict as he began to cry. As soon as he was able to say his child's name, he whispered in my ear, "Billy died this past July."

"I know," I said. "Why don't you come into the office and let's have coffee together?"

The first thing I said when we sat down was, "Tell me what happened." And he told me the story. Telling the story helps, even when it is still difficult to tell. Then he apologized for crying and confessed that he thought he was "losing it."

"Oh, you're no more losing it than I am," I said with the conviction of one who has heard far too many grieving people confess the same thing. "You are grieving," I continued, "and great grief is the price of great love. I know you love your children very much, and Billy must have been someone special."

He looked up and into my eyes and said, "This is his coat. I like to wear it. I feel close to him when I have it on. Now, how weird is that?"

"Not weird at all. When my daughter was in high school, twelve years after her father died, we found a box in the attic with one of Bob's practice football jerseys in it. She wore that jersey as a nightshirt for years. It was kind of like tangible proof that she had a dad who played football and loved her very much."

"My God, how old was she when he died?"

"Four."

"Was he in an accident?"

"No, he died of cancer nine days after it was diagnosed."

"How did you live through it?" he asked.

"Well, when I was only in the fourth month of life without him, like you are, I didn't think I would, but I did."

And I told him the story.

When I finished he said, "Give me something to do. I need something to do."

"Okay," I replied, "how is your back?"

"My back, what do you mean?"

"Can you dig a hole, maybe a few holes?"

"Sure."

"Good, because we need to start a memorial garden for Carolyn. Weeping Pine Nursery is going to donate some shrubs, and the PSO is donating bulbs. We need to get this stuff in the ground before it freezes. I have my hands rather full here, running the school and helping these teachers help the students through this, so I need help. This is a great project, because these kids are hurting, too. They miss her. And having a place where they can plant things to honor her will give them 'something to do,' and I don't have to tell you how important that is."

"No, ma'am," he said with new conviction in his voice, as he stood and pulled out his wallet. "You'll need good dirt and fertilizer and peat moss and, well, how much do you need?"

"Well, right now I don't know, but I'll let you know. And, hey, I have a great idea. Let's put an evergreen of some kind in this garden for Billy. We can put a little plaque on it or in the ground with his name on it, too. It will be Mrs. Small's special memorial, and we can honor others who have died who are a part of the Traphagen School family along with her."

The next day and in the following weeks Bob Foschini did exactly what I asked. He coordinated the project, donated a bird bath, contributed funds for the "extras" and dropped by to tell me more about Billy's life. He volunteered to help me with a student whose mother had died and was "acting out" his grief in rather destructive ways. People love seeing Bob Foschini come into the schools. They trust him. They also have ached for him and wanted to help. Now, he is helping us . . . in memory of Billy . . . and we are all finding comfort in this mutual endeavor.

A present grief can have the effect of a chain reaction in reverse, pulling to the present moment all of the grief and losses in our lives. Often it is so strong, it weakens us. Some say it feels like being sucked back in those previous times

and emotions. I wonder why in the swirling vortex of unresolved grief, we seldom remember the comfort. Does the
pain and isolation trump all other memories?

WEEK TWO

It seems we got back to some business-as-usual this week.
Most of the food and flowers were gone. Reports had to be
filed, tests administered. The irritation of some people getting on other people's nerves became evident, because we
tend to handle grief differently. The ones who tried to focus
on the work at hand irritated the ones who wanted to talk
about memorial gardens and putting her picture on book-
marks for everyone. People found allies who were more like
them and murmured a little about the "others." So, I figured
it was time for a faculty meeting.

We met in the library, and everyone hoped for brevity
and a low emotional charge or tone to the interaction. I
went through some mundane scheduling issues and
announcements, until I felt people relax. A couple of teachers engaged in typical bantering with each other, and we all
laughed. Then I said, "Before we go, we need to talk for a
minute about Carolyn and this grief experience. I believe
we are all more alike than we are different, when we go
through times like this, but we sure handle it differently.
This has more to do with how we were taught, the models
we have had and the circumstances of our personal lives.
But, what I have learned about grief is that the willingness
to process it, however that may be, is key. And there are
some strange emotions to process, like guilt. I know that
some of you feel like your mentor and guiding force is gone
from your life, and you wish you could have told her one

more time how much you appreciated her. I also know that she was a strong-minded woman with definite ideas about the 'right way' to do things and if you did not agree with her it might have driven you crazy. You might not have liked her. You might have wished her gone." As I said this I felt like everyone was holding his or her breath. No one moved.

"However," I continued, "no one wanted her dead. No one wished for her life to end in this untimely, tragic way." By this time every eye was on me, as if they wondered if I would turn into a pillar of salt for what I was saying, but I went on. "Guilt is an incredible thing. It can be a prime motivator in our lives, driving us on to great feats or depths to which we might never go without it. But it is a loose cannon that needs a strong hand, lest it go off into some place you don't want it to go. You may have admired Carolyn and never told her. You may have desired to follow the standards she had set for the school and failed. You may not have felt that way at all and zealously dug in your oppositional heels. All of this conjures up guilt. Guilt is like something we keep tripping over. And what we need to do is to examine it and know it for exactly what it is, a normal human reaction. Once we acknowledge it, we can take our guilt and all of the other normal grief reactions we have and use them. Build on them. Let them motivate us, rather than be controlled by them."

I think all of that took about one and a half minutes to say, maybe two, but it seemed like an eternity. "Does that make sense?" I asked. They all nodded. "Good. Now let's get on with it. Have a nice evening and come back tomorrow, and we'll do it all over again." Someone asked if we had to, and everyone chuckled as we adjourned. The reaction the next day to our meeting was incredible. I think some people

thought I was going to force them into an emotionally
wrenching process or group catharsis and make them
answer that odious question "How do you feel?" They
seemed relieved that I didn't make them "do" anything, yet
the overwhelming feedback was that we "did something
important together."

The ability to acknowledge grief is in all of us. I don't know
why we act like it is this sacred thing that no one should
address. I felt kind of like the kid who said the emperor was
wearing no clothes. I only stated the obvious. In this case, I
was saying what is there in all of us, and that's the human
spirit, which aches when we are hurt, like we bleed when we
are cut. Normal human emotions, when honored and
acknowledged, can bring comfort because we feel more
"comfortable" in our similarities than in our differences. And
we all like to feel comfortable. The pain of grief washes over
us with guilt, regret, longing and sadness. And that makes us
uncomfortable. But those same waves of grief wash up
memories that can bring a sweet taste to life, create warm
feelings and bring honor to those who have "gone on" from
among us.

The next day I began having similar conversations in the
classrooms.

END OF WEEK TWO

It's difficult to do this work when you are tired. On this
evening I was tired, on a plane, flying home, aching to crawl
into bed . . . my bed. Instead, I was sitting on the runway at
LaGuardia, waiting for air traffic control to let us take off.
Angry that we were just sitting there, I wanted to yell
out to someone to "move the bloomin' plane." I had been

with teachers, students, parents, colleagues, newspaper reporters, family and friends processing this stuff all week.
And that's tiring.

We were all tired. Grief does that. It feels like those heavy
lead aprons the dental hygienist puts on you prior to x-raying
your teeth. And after you have worn that for a couple of
weeks it wears on you. The urge to separate, to get away, to
not talk, to fall into a malaise kept pulling at the corners of
my mind.

I had joked with people this week, saying that I was taking up a new career, perhaps in the culinary arts. They'd
smile a little and say, "I don't blame you," and then they
would suggest that the only emotional problems I would
have to deal with is overcooking, or using the wrong herb,
or a fallen soufflé.

"Sounds good to me," I said, and I realized we had begun
joking with each other a little, even using some gallows
humor. One day as I left school, someone reminded me that
the wet leaves on the streets made the road slippery. And
someone else said sarcastically, "Oh, that's just what we
need, 'next principal in car accident.'" A couple of people
"booed" at the comment, but all of us laughed. And I was
reminded anew of how much laughter helps, but it's got to
come from within the circle of those who share the loss and
grief in common. It was still too fresh, too raw, for someone
else to make a joke. Perhaps later.

The pain of grief intensifies when the shock and denial
wear off, and that is what happened for all of us during this
week. We were angrier than normal and frustrated about
the little things. The flowers had died and all that we had left
were vases with scummy dirt that wouldn't wash out. Even
the kids seemed tired. I didn't hear any conversations about

what they were wearing for Halloween, but at least they were talking, asking questions. "Will Mrs. Small's spirit come back on Halloween?" "Tell me again what happened when her car rolled over." "Can she see us?" One little boy handed in another leaf for Mrs. Small's tree. It said,

Dear Mrs. Small,

My little brother, Michael, is in heaven. Maybe you could teach him to read.

No matter how kids act, they are thinking about it.

When I left school at the end of the day, I saw three or four little girls doing a cheer on the sidewalk outside of the office, but they stopped when they saw me, perhaps thinking cheerleading might be disrespectful. I smiled at them, while I read their minds, and said, "Hey, that's a good idea. We all need a little cheering up, don't we?" They nodded and eagerly resumed the hand motions that fit the chant. I marveled at their energy.

I knew this all was important, but I had forgotten how hard it is. I have new understanding today of why we have developed the "get over it, get on with it" strategy in our society.

WEEK THREE

I went into the All-Purpose Room at noontime when its purpose was lunch. The tables were set up and kids were eating and talking and anxiously waiting for the time when they could go out to the playground. I walked around and talked to them and the lunch aides and handled a discipline problem between a couple of overly physical boys. It was all typical principal stuff. And I realized how important it is that someone keeps doing the "jobs" that need to be done when someone dies. The people who are grieving often do not have the energy to do their own jobs, let alone the jobs left behind by the one who is gone. I realized this when I spoke to Carolyn's daughter, Anne, earlier in the day and she was discouraged. I asked what was going on and she said, "The house is a wreck."

"How so?" I inquired. "Does it need to be cleaned?"

"No," she said, "it isn't that. It's just . . . I don't know. I don't seem to have energy to do anything. Mother would have had all of these articles in frames; collages made of the pictures, scrapbooks overflowing with the letters, cards and photographs. And I can't seem to do anything. She would have collected pictures and sent them to everyone who was hurting, and I am having difficulty writing notes."

"Well . . . ," I said, and kind of left the word hanging.

So she went on, "Do you know what I found today? I found the poems she wrote after her mother died. She wrote poems. I don't know. . . ."

The implied message in her "I don't know . . ." was "I don't know what's wrong with me."

So, I asked her, "Do you remember me telling you that grief drains us of our energy and our ability to focus and the motivation to do stuff?"

She did not reply.

"Well, this is a perfect example," I continued, as though she had answered affirmatively. "I think it's enough that on some days you get up and take a shower and get dressed. Going on takes tremendous energy, but I think it would take even more energy trying to be your mom."

"Well, I could never do that; she was incredible," she said with such longing in her voice.

I suggested she come over to the school and sit with me in her mom's office.

"But I'm not dressed. Actually I'm not even up," she rebutted.

"Good," I said, "perfect timing. Get out of bed, throw on some sweats and get over here."

"But, I'm not showered."

"Okay, so you'll sit on the other side of the desk."

We both chuckled.

In the office, sitting on the flowered cushions of her mother's wicker office furniture, she wept and told me how miserable this all was, and, of course, I agreed with her.

"Tell me what your mother would want you to do," I suggested.

"I don't know. I don't seem to know anything anymore," she replied and wiped away her tears with a tissue. "I just don't know."

"Well, answer me this: Would your mother want you to try to become her or would she want you to be your own person, which, incidentally, has some of her in there with you?"

She looked over at me with a tiny sparkle in her beautiful dark eyes, and said, "That's a loaded question if I ever heard one."

"Well, of course it is," I replied, "but it, nonetheless, needs to be answered. And you know the answer. She was so proud of how you have grown and who you are, and she marveled at your talent. That's why she hung the portrait you painted of the two of you in her office. 'Look at what my talented daughter can do. I don't know where she got all of this talent. Certainly not from me,' she told me one day when I complimented her on the painting. She thought you were becoming an incredible person all on your own, and I think she would be furious with you if you quit. She lost her mother when she was sixteen, and she experienced firsthand what this horrible lethargy is like. It seems to affect everyone at one time or another while we are grieving. But I'll bet you all the money I have in the bank she did not stop being Carolyn; she was far too stubborn for me to imagine that."

We both smiled at the truth of her stubbornness.

"You alone can be you, and you can only do the best you can right now. It will get better in time, and you will be able to do more. Here's what's important about doing things: prioritize. You can't do it all. You may not even be able to do much, but do what you can, because not doing anything is dangerous," I said.

"What do you mean?" she asked.

"Depression is a normal reaction to grief for many of us. It draws us into the lie that there is nothing we can do to change back the clock, so why do anything? It is easier to withdraw, pleading the need to rest. And people let us, out of respect, of course. Then we stay in bed and don't return calls because they take too much energy. We get sick of having the same conversations with everyone, so it is easier not to talk. We get discouraged because we can't seem to finish a task, so why start at all? We feel irritated with some of the people who are trying to help, so we disconnect to spare their feelings. And by this time the thought of doing anything is more than we can contemplate. Sound familiar?"

She nodded her head.

"The reason you need to 'do' anything—work, dishes, go out with friends, whatever—is to keep you involved, connected. That way you don't slip into that downward spiral we know as depression, because getting out of there definitely takes more energy than staying connected. And don't layer some heavy agenda on yourself about what you *should* be doing. Just do whatever you can."

WEEK SIX

Today I went into a fifth-grade class and the teacher had already told the children that I was going to come and that we were going to talk some more about what we all had experienced together after Mrs. Small's death. So there was a kind of quietness that came over the class when I walked in, even though these were the same kids I had been with on the playground the day before, and they were anything but quiet. I put a student chair that was low in the front of the room so I could sit close, with them on the floor in front of me. I called them by groups and they came quietly and sat mostly with their legs crossed. These little ten- and eleven-year-old faces looked up at me, and I knew they were eager. They were ready. They are just so much less reticent than we adults are to talk about this.

Also, on this day a newspaper reporter was with us from the *New Jersey Bergen Record*. He had started an article on me in September, with a focus of "Local Principal Leaves to Do Grief Work," and now interestingly this article would be something like, "Local Principal Comes Back to Do Grief Work." He sat in the back of the room with his notepad at a table. The children eyed him curiously. I decided that it would be better for me to introduce him to the class, so I did. The children all said "hello," and then they turned back around and settled down.

I said to them, "Let's talk some more about Mrs. Small and what it's been like for us since she died." I did not say, "passed away," because I think that it is refreshing to children to have an adult be honest with them. I said, "Let's talk for a few minutes about what it is you miss. What in the last couple of weeks have you found yourself feeling, you know that feeling inside that sort of longs to see her face again, to hear her voice? What is it?" Hands shot up in the air. The first child said, "I miss going into her office and seeing all of her bears." Another child said, "I miss all the funny things that she wore." Another one said, "I miss the fact that she was always trying to help us solve problems." And I said, "You know, let's start listing some of these things."

I turned around and once again took up the teacher's magic wand, a piece of chalk. I handed it to each child to write on the chalkboard some of the things they missed. They were all the qualities and attributes of her life and the things she shared with them: the special moments, the celebrations, the problems. The students talked about how much they loved the way she had been real serious about teaching them character values, like honesty, caring, compassion and responsibility. Someone asked if we were going to continue doing that. And I said, "Sure, and let's list what else she would want us to continue." So, they listed some more things like, "She taught us how to be caring and friendly and how to volunteer for things," and we made this wonderful list on the board.

As I had done before with other groups of children, we went through this list item by item. As we went along I asked, "Can you be friendly? Can you have a warm, wonderful smile for everyone? Can you be inviting and including the way she was? Can you help people solve problems? Can you be honest? Can you show compassion? Can you show caring?" I went through this wonderful exercise with them where I showed them that all of the very things they loved about this principal who was no longer with them were the things she had given to them. These things they now owned.

Next I said, "I want you to look at this list and see if there's anything that she did that you can't do." One student said, "I can't be principal." And I said, "Well, what if you went to college and went to graduate school and majored in educational administration and got your principal's license? Could you be a principal?" And of course this little boy said, "Well, yeah, I guess I could." I looked back to catch the eye of the reporter to see if he was "with" us, and he was not sitting at the table. I wondered if I had become so involved, so engrossed that I didn't notice him leave the room. Then I saw some movement in an aisle between the desks, and I realized that he was sitting in the back of the group, that he had joined us. I smiled warmly at him and thought again of how refreshing it is to be an adult sitting among children and listening to their honest interactions, probing questions and thoughtful reflections. I wondered when was the last time he had done that.

I went on with the exercise for a while and then asked this group of ten- and eleven-year-olds a question. If I had them stand up and walk out of this classroom with me and go to a first-grade class, would they be able to teach our first-graders what they have learned about all that was given to them by Mrs. Small? I asked them if they could describe the different characteristics of someone who is caring, honest, cooperative or responsible, and what I really wanted to know was if they thought they could teach them. A couple of them shook their heads "no," and a

couple shrugged their shoulders, but the majority of them
began to kind of nod their heads affirmatively, like, "Yeah,
I could probably teach a first-grader how to be honest and
what it means to be responsible."

To the ones who had shaken their heads "no" I said,
"What was your favorite thing of all these things on this
list? Look up here at this list." And one of them said that
Mrs. Small was always helping them find ways to solve
their problems. I said, "Okay, now here you are with a
group of first-graders on the playground, and they are fighting over the kickball. One group says, 'The other group has
had it long enough,' and this group says, 'We had it first,'
and they're fighting. Tell me how you'd solve that." So this
little fifth-grade girl laid out her strategy. She said that she
would sit down with them and talk to them about how much
time they had left for recess. Then she would explain that
the only fair thing to do was: If there were eight minutes left
in recess, one group could use the ball for four minutes and
then the other group could use it for four minutes and each
group would cheer for the other group while they were
playing. I told her I thought that was a wonderful lesson.

Then I looked in her face and said, "Do you really think
you can do that?"

She said, "Yes, I do."

I said, "So you could teach first-graders these wonderful
qualities that Mrs. Small taught you?"

She nodded again. I continued, "Now, it takes practice to
do these things. It even takes practice for adults. But if we
do this, if we take these wonderful qualities that we loved so
in Mrs. Small, and that we miss so much, and we bring them
to life in our life, will a part of her be living on in us?" They
agreed as a group that she would. "And could we keep that

for a long time? Do you think we could keep those qualities for a few weeks, a couple of months?"

Someone said, "Years, if we want to."

I said, "Okay, how about the rest of your life?"

They thought they could, but they would definitely need to practice. One child said they'd all probably have to do something to remember those qualities. And I said, "In remembering those things, who else would you be remembering?" And of course they knew. And I said to them, "You know I've spent a lot of time over the past fifteen years working with people who are grieving and talking to families who are hurting the way our little school family has been hurting and even working with people who were dying. And while I didn't get a chance to ask Mrs. Small about this, I'll tell you what we know about people who are dying, who are sick and know they are going to die. We know what their number-one fear is. Anybody have any idea what that would be? If you spent a lot of time in hospitals where people were dying, what do you think their number-one fear is?" They thought, and they puzzled, and they thought, but that was too big a stretch for them. I guess maybe they are too alive to think about what they would be afraid of if they were looking death in the face personally. So I told them that the number-one fear dying people have is that they will be forgotten. They fear that two years later or five years later nobody would remember that they were here, nobody will say their name. Nobody will talk about the good times and the hard times, the things they did that made other people's lives better, the way we laughed, the way we cried together. Then I said, "If we remember what Mrs. Small taught us, if we live the kind of life that she did, with all these wonderful qualities you liked so much, and if we teach this to others, can we remember her for the rest of our lives?" They agreed. "Can you, when you're old enough to tell your grandchildren about these very things, still remember Mrs. Small? Will you be keeping a part of her with you for the rest of your lives?"

They agreed. I reminded them that Christa McAuliffe, the teacher who died in the Challenger explosion, said, "To teach is to touch the future." And so, we can take all that we admired about Mrs. Small with us into the future of our lives. "Does that mean we'll quit missing her?" I answered my own question, "Over time that'll get a little easier, but do we forget her? No!

"This hurt that we feel right now will ease up. It will not be as painful to remember her a year from now, five years from now or when we have grandchildren.

"How does that feel?"

Everyone said, "Good."

Week Ten

Three children visited my office this week: a first-grade girl, a fourth-grade boy and a fifth-grade girl. Two of the children were referred by their parents, the other one by his teacher.

A Fifth-Grade Girl Grieves Her Losses

Susan, a fifth-grade student, was failing in her school-work and didn't seem to care. Her parents were worried about her lethargy and lack of interest in general, neither of which was typical for Susan. Her dad and I had worked together the year before on a district committee, so he felt comfortable calling me. This reinforced in me the belief that the members of the Grief and Loss team need to be those who are trusted by the general public, because they have a record of caring for and working successfully with kids.

Now this dad was wondering if his daughter might be grieving. Mrs. Small had called on Susan a number of times when she was putting together skits for school assemblies, and he thought Susan might be missing her and not talking about it. He had tried having a discussion with her, but she rebuffed all attempts. He also told me he had started a new job, with a long commute, and he did not get home until 7:30 or 7:45 in the evening. So, he felt like there was never a good time to get to the bottom of this with his daughter. When I hung up the phone I remembered seeing this family at the holiday concert at the high school. The mom was proudly introducing everyone to the family's newest foster baby, a beautiful little three-month-old girl.

I spoke with Susan's teacher. She had held a conference the previous day with Susan's mom, and both were concerned about her plummeting grades and indifference. So, I set up a time for Susan to come to my office. When she came in, we talked for a little while about Mrs. Small, what they did together, and how strange it feels that she isn't coming back. Then I told her that everyone was concerned about her and asked if she knew why. She shrugged her shoulders and turned her face slightly away. Since she didn't seem to pick up on my attempts to discuss Mrs. Small or her plummeting grades, I decided to ask her about her family's plans for the holidays.

Her face lit up. "We are going to get to visit Jessie," she exclaimed. This was more energy than I had seen before, so I asked for details, beginning with, "Who is Jessie?" It seems this family had taken in a foster baby during the past year named Jessie. For Susan, it was love at first sight. She was animated in her descriptions of him as a baby, learning to crawl, his first words, etc. If I closed my eyes I could have imagined that she was a proud grandparent smitten with a first grandchild. Then she told me of her family's efforts to adopt Jessie, which were about to be accomplished, when Jessie's grandmother appeared on the scene and was given preference by the courts as his adoptive parent. Jessie now lives with his grandmother. Susan and her family were terribly disappointed.

"So, let's see," I said, looking up at the ceiling like I was computing a math problem in my head. "In the last two months, you have lost Jessie and Mrs. Small, right?"

She nodded.

"And your dad, who used to help you with your homework, doesn't get home now until it's almost time for you to go to bed."

She looked at me like I was a psychic, and I whispered, "Your dad told me."

"Oh," she said, with a downward inflection, realizing I had spoken with her father.

"And," I continued, "I think I remember seeing a new baby on your mom's shoulder at the concert, didn't I?"

This brought a small smile to her face, but it vanished quickly, as she realized all she was going through.

"So, Mom doesn't have quite as much time for you since the baby came, does she?"

Susan had knotted into a little ball the tissue I had given her earlier and she dabbed it at her eyes.

"These are all hard things, aren't they?"

She nodded and squeezed her tissue-ball in one hand and made a fist.

"I want you to know you are right. These are hard things. And you have had a lot of them all at once, and that makes it even harder to handle."

No response.

"So, I guess you could sort of feel like giving up on some things, like homework, huh?"

She looked up at me to see if there was scorn in my eyes. When she saw none, she agreed.

"Well, I've felt that way a little bit myself this week. It seems like I just don't have the energy to keep my mind on what I am doing. I feel like I start a lot of things, but don't seem to finish very many . . . ," I said.

I could feel her looking at me, but I continued staring at the far wall, wanting this to sink in—wanting her to know that we all go through a crazy mixture of emotions when we are grieving, when what we have counted on gets turned upside down.

"Yeah," she said, so softly I could barely hear her. "I can't seem to remember anything my teacher says."

"Hmmm," I replied, and waited awhile. Then I said, "I wonder, if you told her this, if maybe she might find some ways to help you. What do you think?"

"Yeah, she probably would. She's nice."

"Well, that's one idea, but I guess we probably need some more, and since neither one of us is thinking too clearly, where do you suggest we go?"

"I don't know," she replied too quickly.

"Well, why don't you think about it and I'll think about it, and we can talk again tomorrow."

"Okay," she said and seemed a little relieved. "Can I go to art class now?"

"Sure," I said, smiling, and held my trash basket out so she could dunk her tissue-ball.

She left the office with somewhat better posture than she had upon entering. Maybe the only thing she gained was understanding, but that goes a long way. Most of us know there are no shortcuts, and problems usually take more than a day to solve. But she had a new person in her corner when she left school that day, and I knew she would be back.

A Fourth-Grade Boy Shares the Death of His Grandfather

Tony's teacher was concerned about his lack of interest, not only in his work but also with his friends and in any of the school activities. This reminded me of how helpful the home and school relationship can be for providing each other with information. Quick notes between teacher and parent in a book bag or backpack can cover a lot of territory. That is how this information was exchanged. When both sides ran out of ideas they decided to send him to me. By this time, I had been in the school for almost three months and people were starting to tap into me as a trusted resource. Trust is key here. We arranged a time for Tony to come to my office.

I asked him if he had ever been in Mrs. Small's office, and he said he had. "Does it look the same?" I asked him. He nodded his head as his eyes scanned the space and then came back to me. "Except I am here, not Mrs. Small, right?" He nodded. I told him I was sorry that this was changing and explained that I was spending a lot of time helping the district find a new principal. I explained that Mrs. Small and I had been friends and that I would do everything I could to help find a wonderful person for the job.

"But, there will never be another Mrs. Small, will there?" I affirmed, tapping into his thoughts.

He shook his head negatively, looking down at his lap.

"We can find other people to do a person's job, work in the person's office, sometimes even live in the person's home. . . ." I let that thought hang in the air a little while and then said, "But no one ever takes another person's place in our lives. I'm here being the principal of your school, but even if I were here for the next ten years, I would never be Mrs. Small, would I?"

"And no one can ever take my grandfather's place either. Ever!" he offered and squeezed his eyes shut, trying to prevent tears from spilling out.

"Heavens no!" I exclaimed. Then I said, "Tell me about your grandfather."

A sentence starting with "Tell me about . . ." that is spoken with matter-of-fact sincerity can yield valuable insights that direct questions/answers might not evoke.

"He died right before Thanksgiving," he offered.

"Oh, Tony, I'm so sorry. I'll bet Thanksgiving was tough." He nodded his head.

"Is your grandmother living?"

Another nod.

"I'll bet she is glad to have you around, isn't she?"

"They . . . I mean, she lives in New York State, so we don't get to see her real often, and she doesn't even know how to ski."

"Ski?" I said, wondering how many grandmothers do ski, yet knowing that all information is important, I asked the first logical question that came to me.

"Did you ski with your grandfather?"

"Oh, yeah. He was a very famous man at Lake Placid. He was a timer at the Winter Olympics there. He even shot off the starting gun. And everyone there knew him. And every Christmas we'd go up there, and he got lift passes for all of us and we skied every day. And now . . ."

"You aren't going to be able to ski this Christmas, are you?" I finished his sentence.

"Well, not there. My grandfather got us in. He was a very important man, and he got lift passes for us because he worked there."

"So, you skied on the same runs that Olympic skiers raced?"

"Yeah. It was really cool. I couldn't go down the black runs though, only the blue ones."

"Wow, that's incredible. Have any of your friends ever skied there?"

"No, but now I won't either."

"But you did, more than once, didn't you? And I'll bet you'll never forget it, will you?"

He thought about that a minute.

"And," I continued, "I'll bet you remember that for the rest of your life. I'll even bet that every time you go skiing anywhere, you'll think about skiing with your grandfather at Lake Placid. I can just see you when you have kids of your own, watching TV and seeing something from Lake Placid, and saying to them, 'Hey, I used to ski there with my grandfather when I was a kid.' What do you think they'll say?"

"They probably won't believe me."

"So, you'll have to tell them all about your grandfather and the important job he had there."

"He was famous. Everyone said 'hi' to him everywhere we'd go."

"You're a lucky guy to have had him for your grandfather."

I let that sink in a moment, then I asked, "Do you know what a memory is?"

"Yeah."

"What is it?"

"It's thinking about something that happened."

"Like skiing with your grandfather."

"Yeah."

"How long can you remember that, like how many years?"

"I don't know. I guess as long as I want to."

"You're right. And even if you never ski there again, but I bet you will someday, you can remember it for the rest of your life. And your grandfather gave you those memories, didn't he? And you know what else he gave you? Genes. Do you know what genes are?"

"Yeah, they're what makes you tall or short or have blue eyes or brown eyes."

"And a lot of other things, too. That's the stuff we inherit from our parents and grandparents and great-grandparents. So you have some of your grandfather in you right now, and you will always have that with you. And you are probably going to be just as great a man as he was."

Tony kind of shrugged that off, but I knew he was thinking about it. So I went on trying to bring my point home.

"Did you know that Mrs. Small came to visit me in my home in Indiana?"

"No."

"Well, she did, and she had never been there before and didn't know what to expect. And she wanted to do everything. I have a picture of her sitting in the driver's seat of a tractor and even a big combine. She had a ball and loved learning everything about life on the farm." I was smiling and chuckling at the memory. "Sounds just like something she would do, doesn't it?"

Tony agreed.

Then I said, "I don't think I will ever see a tractor now without thinking of my friend, Carolyn Small. I can close my eyes and almost see her there."

I hoped Tony was connecting his ability to remember with my remembering.

"And even though it makes me feel sad when I realize she will never come out for another visit, I would rather think about her than forget her. That would be awful."

Tony said nothing, so I went on, "Just like it would be awful to forget your grandfather, wouldn't it?"

"I'd never do that," he determined.

"Of course not," I said, and our eyes met almost like we were promising each other we would never forget.

"But you have to practice remembering. Do you know some ways to do that?"

"No."

"Oh, sure you do. You just did it. You were remembering your grandfather. And what did you do? Did you think about it all by yourself?"

"No, I told you."

"So, that's one way to practice. You also could write about him. How about the next time you have a writing assignment, when you get to pick the topic, writing about your grandfather? Or, maybe you could draw a picture in art class sometime of Lake Placid or skiers. That's another way to practice. And when you are having a happy memory, it somehow makes the sadness of losing them easier to handle. Know what I mean?"

"Yeah," he said, almost smiling.

"I think it's easiest for me to practice remembering by telling someone about it, so I'm sure glad you came by so we could talk about them for awhile. I feel better."

"Yeah," he said, "me, too."

A First-Grader Misses Her Principal

Amanda's mother sent me a note. She was worried because Amanda was still crying almost every day over Mrs. Small's death; Amanda's mother wondered if I could help. I called her back and said I would love to see her and her daughter. I tried to gather some background information while we were talking and asked if Amanda's grandparents were living. They were. I asked if they had lost any pets. They had not. I asked if they had moved recently and that wasn't a factor either. Then I asked the mom if she and her husband were talking about this with Amanda. She said they talked about it daily, because almost every morning Amanda would say she did not want to go to school. She would say something like she had a stomachache or some other reason, but mostly it all boiled down to the fact that Mrs. Small would not be there. I asked this mom how they had handled the pertinent information about death, and they had done a great job. They had read Amanda all of the books recommended by the Crisis Management Team for her age level. Since I couldn't think of anything else to suggest, we arranged for them to stop in the office after school the next afternoon. They came hand in hand, looking like they were treading on sacred ground.

Now, Carolyn Small had about twenty bears in her office, so the first thing I did when Amanda and her mother came in was suggest that Amanda find her two favorite bears and hold them while we talked. One of the bears was wearing a yellow rain slicker. She looked at the tag on its ear and said his name was Gordon. Then she told me that it was her favorite. I asked why. She told me that when she was just a little girl, in kindergarten, last year, she had been afraid to go to school and the first day she cried all morning. I told her that lots of time that happens, especially when it's going to school for the first time and going all alone.

"That's the part that scared me," she said.

"What part was that?" I asked.

"Well, the part that was most scary was going from Mommy's car into the school," she pointed out with widened eyes.

"Why was that the hardest?" I inquired casually, not wanting her to stop talking.

"Well, there were so many other really big kids there, all hurrying and being really loud," she tried to replay the situation for me.

So I said, "Yes, uh huh, it's kind of like that during morning arrival, you're right. And is that what scared you, the loud big kids?"

"Uh huh, 'cause they were all going so many different ways that I was scared, until Mrs. Small helped me," she explained.

"Oh, tell me about that. I love to hear about everything Mrs. Small did. She was wonderful, wasn't she?"

"Oh, yes," she sighed, as she hugged the yellow-slickered bear.

I also realized in the moment that Gordon was going to have a new home at Amanda's house.

"So, tell me what she did," I begged, leaning forward with my elbows on my knees and my chin on my folded hands.

"Well, it was raining. I remember because I had on my raincoat, and I was scared to get out of the car," she recalled. "But Mrs. Small was standing out in the rain with her duck umbrella, opening car doors so the kids could get out. When she opened our door I was crying, and she asked me if I would come into her office. Mama said I could, so we came in here, and she asked me what I was scared of, so I told her."

"What did you say?" I asked, as if I couldn't wait to hear the rest of the story.

"Well," she continued, "I told her about all of the kids and that I was scared that I might get lost or get knocked down or maybe even get pushed out in the street."

I thought about the broad sidewalk where she arrives at school that leads directly to the kindergarten and couldn't imagine any harm coming her way. But simultaneously, I knew that school phobia is usually based more in fear than reality.

"So, what did Mrs. Small say?" I asked her.

"She said she was going to give me Sara."

"A bear?" I asked, probably because I was thinking about giving her the bear in her hands.

"No," she giggled, "Sara isn't a bear; she's a girl! She's a Kindergarten Guardian."

"Of course," I giggled with her. "I know about them; they are special members of the school patrol team, right?"

"Yes, and Mrs. Small gave me my own guardian. That's Sara."

"So, let me guess. Every time you come to school, Sara greets you and opens the door of your car and walks you to your class, right?"

"No, not anymore," she proudly asserted, "I'm a big girl now. I'm in first grade."

"Of course, but that's how you got over being scared last year, isn't it?"

"Yes, and Mrs. Small told me that if I was ever scared again to come in and tell her about it, and now I can't. . . ."

Big elephant tears slid down her cheeks.

This may have been one of the most honest, uncomplicated expressions of grief I have ever seen. It wasn't tied to anything else. It was plainly and simply a six-year-old grieving the loss of her gracious and wonderful principal, who had helped her and given her confidence and now was gone forever.

"You know what, Amanda, Mrs. Small was absolutely right," I reached over and took her hand. She looked up into my eyes and I continued, "She told you that when you are scared you need to tell someone you trust and that person will help you. It actually helps to talk about it. Somehow things are not as scary when we talk about them, are they? Once you told her, it got better, didn't it? But I wonder what would have happened if you hadn't told her. You might still be scared. Right? So talking about things helps us find ways to solve them, doesn't it?"

I patted Amanda's hand and asked her if she knew how much Mrs. Small loved bears. She said she knew that. Then I said, "You know that bear in the yellow slicker kind of reminds me of Mrs. Small's duck umbrella. It was yellow, too, wasn't it?"

"Yes," she said, holding the bear out in front of her to see the similarity for herself.

"Well, I have a great idea. Why don't you take this rain bear home with you to remind you of all that Mrs. Small taught you?"

"Could I?" she asked, looking at her mother, who nodded affirmatively.

"You can put this rain bear next to your bed and any time you are feeling a little sad, or even scared, you can tell Mrs. Small's bear. How's that for a good idea? And every time you do that I bet you will think of Mrs. Small, won't you?"

Amanda hugged her bear and crossed her heart and promised me she would do so.

I used to think that things like worry stones were silly. I don't think so anymore.

When they left, I went to Carolyn's shelves behind the desk and pulled out her yellow umbrella with the duck face painted on the top and its orange bill flopping over the edge. I could see it sheltering a scared little kindergartener and her rescuing principal.

Carolyn's story and the grief experienced by her faculty, staff and students provide us with a snapshot of the ways in which a grief and loss team can intervene, comfort and encourage. I continue to go into her school monthly, not only to do this grief work, but also to provide a transition for the new administration. As I write these pages, I wish we had trained a team to do this a year ago. So I encourage all educators who are considering putting this book into action to do so now. When the inevitable losses confront your school community, you will be grateful you are prepared.

Part II

Stories

A New Approach

Grief takes place over time, even over a lifetime. While it does not take place all the time, it surfaces intermittently, sometimes unpredictably. It seldom fits anyone's schedule. It typically includes a powerful, often overwhelming, combination of reactions, with emotional, psychological, spiritual, intellectual and physical components. The experience differs from person to person since the variables of age, resources, health and other personal circumstances are different. For students at different developmental stages of growth the differences are great, but the descriptions given by most include similarities, like pain, remorse, injustice, anger, longing, fear, despair, panic, regret, guilt, sadness, futility, aching and confusion, to name a few.

When Elisabeth Kubler-Ross introduced her stages in *On Death and Dying*, she noted having observed similar stages of responses in the grieving families of her dying patients. I am not sure it was ever her intention for these stages to be applied as broadly and emphatically to the grieving process as has occurred. Her seminal work and many others that followed have gained popularity in the self-help literature as prescriptives for getting over grief. While her famous stages of grief are a helpful framework, they are often rigidly applied by others to the grieving, who are then urged to get to the last stage of "acceptance" as quickly as possible. This unrealistic expectation then becomes a burden to the grieving rather than a framework for understanding what is happening to them. Any stage, step or "how-to" plan for us who are grieving needs the accompanying philosophy or understanding that some losses last a lifetime.

What I have heard from grieving people, both inside and outside of school, over the last twenty-five years is that they want to know "how to live with it." The clinical or medical approach is often presented as a prescription for the "others" or patients or clients and lacks the capacity to address the matter for all of us, which is crucial to serving and helping the grieving. In addition, it focuses narrowly on loss by death and does not include other losses often felt with enormous power. Grief is an intensely personal dimension of our lives, and any contact that does not respect that fact should not be made.

The following true stories represent some of the experiences I have had personally with schools and students and parents who were grieving. Some of the schools have expressed interest in training groups of teachers or teams to continue the work we began together. The students in these stories range from first-graders to high school seniors. I offer these stories for the sole purpose of giving insight to the individuals who want to understand and comfort the aggrieved. My heart's desire is to honor the lives of those who have died. Their parents and families allowed me into their hearts and lives during difficult days and have generously encouraged me to tell their stories.

Natalie: A High School Junior

I did not know Natalie, or her sister Ashley, or her parents, Rich and Teresa. Our friend Ken's son, however, was a classmate and close friend of Ashley. So, when Ashley's sister Natalie was killed in a car accident, Ken called and asked if I would help. I said, "Of course," and asked for details. He told me that the parents' main concern was for the kids, Natalie's friends, teammates and classmates, and he wanted to know if I would have time to help some of them. I repeated my willingness, "Of course, I'll do anything I can." Then he told me the story.

Natalie's dad, Rich, is a choral music director in a large area high school, and Friday night was the big Spring Choral Pops Concert. Natalie had left him a note the night before, while he was having the dress rehearsal, asking if she and her friends could take the boat out after school. He had left a reply note saying, "Yes, but you have to wait until I get home, so I can make sure everything is working properly." When he got home around 4:30 P.M., Natalie was not around. So, Rich got the boat ready, changed his clothes and gathered all he needed for the concert that night. He felt badly that he might miss her, but he also knew he could trust her and that she would not take out the boat without his direction. Teresa felt uncomfortable that Natalie had not come home yet, and they were getting ready to leave. She reassured herself with the thought that it was a perfectly beautiful day in late May and track practice may have lasted longer than usual. What neither of them knew was that she had driven a friend to her parents' summer home to pick up a wet suit. They had tried to borrow one from another friend, who must now find it hard to think about his saying "no" when asked, even if it was a logical refusal at the time.

Kosciusko County has more lakes per square mile than most counties in the Midwest. These freshwater lakes, large and small, are the source of great recreation and camping. They are connected by country roads with many criss-crossing intersections, some of which have two-way stops and some of which have four. Natalie and her friend Andrea came to one of those intersections, stopped and then pro-ceeded on through. What happened next is still uncertain. Was the brightness of the setting sun obscuring the truck headed for the same intersection? Did she realize that it was a two-way intersection? Did she see the truck and think it had to stop? Did the driver of the truck see them? Surely those questions were asked again and again, and in reality they do not matter at all. Accidents happen. No one intends them. The only vital question was, "Then what happened?" And the horrible answer is that Natalie was killed. Andrea survived.

Teresa dropped Rich off at the school and had planned to run an errand at a nearby mall before the concert began. But her nagging uneasiness about Natalie being late sent her running into the school to call home. The line was busy. She tried again. And again. Still busy. She found Rich and asked him to keep trying. He said he would and tried a few times. In his mind's eye, he could see one of his daughters chatting happily away on the phone. He busied himself going over all of the equipment for the concert one more time, when the tech director came into his office and said, "There are two police officers out here who want to see you." All of us who work in schools dread these visits, because it usually means one or more of our students are in trouble. It actually went through Rich's mind that there might be a problem in the parking lot, because like all school concerts, this one would be overattended, making parking scarce. When he introduced himself, one of the officers asked if Rich's wife was there. He thought that was odd but answered by saying she would be there shortly. Then the officer asked him if he had a daughter Natalie. He said, "Yes," not wanting to hear any other words. Not wanting another question asked. Wanting to suspend time. But the inevitable words came, "She was killed in an accident on a road over by Lake Tippecanoe." In this time-warp tunnel where shock pulls us, Rich remembered seeing the blue flashing lights of an EMT vehicle on a road between home and school and wondered now if they had been for their daughter. Their youngest. Their Natalie. He turned away from them and picked up the phone, where he had been only moments ago calling home to check on his girls.

Then in the state of "going through the motions" that shock allows us, he called the school principal . . . and band director . . . and assistant principal. He told them all to come. He found his assistant director, Kathy, and told her she would have to take over the concert. There had been an accident. Then he saw Teresa in the doorway. A police officer had approached her in the parking lot. When he asked if she was Rich's wife, she said teasingly, "I suppose you are going to tell me I can't park here." But he said, "No, come with me." And she knew. She was struck walking into the

school, full now of nervous music students with preconcert
jitters, that it was as quiet as a stone. All of the uneasiness
about leaving home before Natalie got there. All of the
motherly intuition. All of the unreasonable worry now made
sense. The police officer pointed for her to go into Rich's
office, and she knew. She knew it was one of her girls. Rich
walked over to her and said, "Natalie has been killed in a
car accident."

When they told me their story, they repeatedly mentioned
the consideration and kindness of the Kosciusko police officers, who gently offered to make calls or drive them home.
They got all of the information that Teresa and Rich asked
them. They followed these newly grieved parents home.
Teresa described the experience by likening it to having a
huge egg on her head, when Rich told her Natalie was dead.
Then the egg cracked and the shock of it all slowly oozed
down her whole body. The ride home felt out of time and
space.

Ashley was home alone. Unaware. Then the doorbell
rang and the coroner stood in the living room and told her
her sister had been killed. No warning. No second chance.
She called one of her mother's best friends, Rena, who is a
nurse. Rena came immediately. The first thing Rich noticed
when he got out of the car at home was the huge oil spot left
by the coroner's car. He wanted it removed. He tried to
wash it out, but it was there for weeks afterward and he
hated it every time he saw it. It seemed odd, but that spot
became emblematic for what they had lost and the audacity
of the messenger who brought the bad news while Rich and
Teresa were not at home.

I got the call sometime over the weekend, inquired about
visitation hours, and slipped into the funeral home feeling

almost like an intruder. I didn't know this family. I saw
Paul, a local youth pastor that I knew, and went over to
speak to him. He said he had been told I would be there and
offered to introduce me to the family. I declined. There
would be time for that later. I looked at all of the teenagers
there and felt badly that I didn't know them. It is difficult to
talk to someone you don't know about something this personal. Before I left quietly, I asked Paul to tell the family I
would be at the funeral and would be happy to speak with
anyone or do anything they wished me to do.

The church was packed. Speakers had been set up in the
church lounge and in some Sunday school rooms. These
teenagers looked like so many I had seen before. I met
Teresa and Rich after the service. Teresa took me by the
hand and said, "There is someone I want you to talk to."
And I met Andy, Natalie's boyfriend. I knew he was in the
same state of shock everyone else was experiencing, so I
gave him my name and phone number, hoping he would
call. Surprisingly he did. So did Teresa. We became friends.

Eventually Teresa and I set up a mutual time to meet
almost weekly. She read everything I suggested, beginning
with the then-unpublished manuscript, *Mourning and
Dancing*. Each week she brought a list of questions to discuss. I suggested that she keep a journal. She had already
started one. She is a bright, committed learner. She wanted
to understand and found no understanding. She sought
logic and found none. She reexamined her theology and
found it sound. Still she was angry. Still the pain was almost
more than she could bear. She came weekly, not for the
answers I gave. We both knew I had no answers, but I was
there. I ached with her. I listened to her. I walked with her
through this dark, all-encompassing place we call grief, and

we became friends. She came to our family's retreat center, where she had never been before Natalie's death, and planted flowers, perennials that would bloom year after year. She is an expert gardener and knew exactly what would grow there. She brought "cuttings" from her garden at home. She grew new things. She worked in the shop and made creative, constructive things.

Teresa and Rich told me that the thing they wanted most, in the first weeks and months after Natalie's death, was for someone who "knew" to tell them they would survive. They wanted to know from someone who had been through it that this pain, this deep hurt, would not pervade their existence forever. That it wouldn't kill them. After all, they had another daughter to raise. I tried to reassure them, but we eventually came to the place where there was a particular reassurance I could not give. After all, I had never lost a child. So, contact was made through a mutual friend with a family whose son had died four or five years earlier. This mother came to their house and sat in their living room and cried. Teresa was told later that this mother had not spoken her son's name in years. When she left they felt worse than ever. In the years that followed, they heard about another family whose child had died, and this family said everything was "fine." God had taken all of their pain away. Within two months of their child's death, this family started a grief group as a business. I wondered what they were saying to people.

Rich and Teresa are people of great faith, and their final conclusion is that believers are not spared the pain of this world. Their faith in God is not a relationship in which they received all the answers, rather it is the source of their strength for going on.

A few months after Natalie died, the son of the football coach in her high school was killed in a car accident. This young man was a college student and was riding home one Friday night to surprise his dad on the night of the big game. This time the call came from Teresa, saying "Sally, you've got to go to the school and help these kids." And, of course, I went. I met with the principal and director of guidance. I suggested that we announce my presence in the morning announcements and tell the kids I would be there all morning if anyone wanted to talk. I asked the principal to encourage kids to come in two's or small groups, mainly because I know how kids relate more to each other than to adults. And they came. In reality I was there all day, through lunch, until 4:30, and I came back the next day. When I walked out of the school with Teresa at 4:30, Rich and Andy were waiting to take her home. They piled in the truck with Andy in the middle and I marveled at the blessing each of them was to the other.

The next day I suggested an evening meeting for parents and kids, so we could talk about grief and how to deal with it. We met in a lecture hall, because the seats were comfortable and the room wasn't too big. Someone suggested the theater, but I declined and explained that a theater is too big, too impersonal, and the speaker is too separated from the audience. It is better to be crowded and close. I also knew that, as much as people want to learn about grief and how to help, it is a difficult subject. It is not unusual when people "intend" to go to a support group or hear a speaker, for something "coincidentally" to come up that seems unavoidable and "prevents" them from going. I had prepared a couple of handouts and a bibliography for the evening. I remember wishing my book had been published, because it was full of real-life stories, designed to help others feel not so alone. I wanted to give it to every person there. Little did I dream that night I would write this story in my second book.

The football coach and his wife (Gene and Carol) were sitting in the front row when I walked into the room with my stacks of papers. I felt weak in the knees. Teresa and Rich were there, too. So were lots of other parents and their children. I swallowed hard, took a drink of water and began.

"I'm sorry to be here tonight with you, but I wouldn't be anywhere else either. My heart aches for the losses you have experienced. I know for most of you the shock of it all has worn off, and you are faced with the realities that none of us ever wanted and all of us fear. When I was twenty-four years old, the man who was my high school sweetheart, eventually my husband and forever the father of my children died. And I wanted to die, too. The pain was too much. The future too bleak. The emptiness unbearable. And nothing can change that. But if it helps at all, twenty-five years have passed, and I am still here and, in particular, I am intentionally here with you. I will not pretend to know your pain or how you feel. I have never lost a child, but I did lose someone I loved with all my heart. No two losses are the same, and no two lives are the same. But I think we are all more alike than we are different. Just like we bleed the same when we are cut, we ache similarly when we suffer loss. How we deal with it, talk about it and find our ways through it are different. I think this has more to do with how we have been raised, what we have been taught and the culture in which we live. But I think pain is pain, and that is what we have in common: the pain of loss in our lives.

Tonight I want to share with you what I have learned over the past twenty-five years. I did some things well and some things quite poorly, and I don't mind sharing it all, because perhaps one piece, one thought will help a little."

When I left later that evening Teresa told me that she and Rich were having Carol and Gene over for dinner the next weekend. I told her how proud I was of all they were doing. They had more guts than I did after Bob died. I spoke with Natalie's boyfriend a few times in the coming months. To this day, he has never lost touch with Teresa and Rich. They opened their home to all of the kids, but after awhile the visits dwindled down to only a few. Teresa feels like she somehow has failed Andrea, who was in the car with Natalie. They don't have any contact at all anymore and still live in the same neighborhood. Grief does strange things to people and much of that we can't control. The only people we can work on and for whom we can be responsible are ourselves. What seems to help most is if we are willing to reach back over the gulf of our own losses and extend our hand to one who is grieving. Then, if they want us to walk with them, healing seems to come.

Michael: An Eighth-Grader

They entered with parents close by, sometimes with a hand on their shoulder. For most of them it was the first time, and, even if they had seen a dead body before, it likely was a grandparent, not a classmate. The curiosity and fear in their eyes betrayed all attempts they made to maintain a cool teenage stoicism that they hoped looked nonchalant.

They looked for the casket and upon finding it looked immediately away, almost like it might be bad luck to look. With furtive glances back at their parents, they scanned the scene, uncertain of what to say or do. Often they stopped in their tracks and had to be urged on, into a receiving line or toward the object of approach/avoidance, their friend's body . . . the body that had been sweating with them last week in the soccer game, the body whose voice had urged them on when the going got rough.

It was unthinkable that his body could be dead, when it was just as alive as they were, only days before. Few on the team even thought about being alive; they just were. Except perhaps, Michael, who only occasionally mentioned his dad, but all who came into the funeral home that night were thinking of Michael's father. Only five years had passed since the out-of-control fire truck had pinned Larry's car against a guardrail and robbed Michael and his brothers of a father, his mother of her husband. And now this unspeakable turn of events made everyone wonder how one family could be asked to endure so much. One week earlier, they had all been together at a Yankees' game eating hot dogs in shorts and sunglasses. Now Michael looked like he had on stage makeup and was lying still in a coffin, those same sunglasses and his favorite hat near by. A tumor in his liver had been slowly eating away at the organ and a vital artery. Violent flu symptoms sent them to the emergency room, but there was nothing anyone could have done. He was dead in an hour. An e-mail message raced across the Internet to his friends, and a stunned community began to mourn.

While circumstances vary, when a child dies, schools and communities across the country scramble to cope, to find some solace, to try to help. And Michael's town was the same. Parents clung to their children, irrationally fearing that Michael's death might be the beginning of a series of tragedies, as though the clutches of death might reach out and grab their children, too. They marveled at his mother's strength, unaware, perhaps, of the numbing effects of shock and denial that accompany trauma and death. But his mother knew this combination of dulling and adrenaline and let it take her through the motions with which she, unfortunately, was all too familiar. She asked a day or two before the wake (that's what the funeral home visits are called in the East) what the family could do to help the children, her other sons and Michael's friends. So we discussed some ideas that, obviously, could be accomplished in a few days. The focus certainly needed to be a way to "involve" the kids, to give them something tangible to do, while trying to deal with the intangible, yet all-consuming, fact that Michael was dead. I also suggested personalized T-shirts would be great if there was a business nearby that could produce a number of shirts with writing on them like "Michael" and "Friends Forever." Then the kids could take permanent markers and sign their names on each other's shirts, and they could all sign one for Michael that could go with him. Construction-paper hearts or soccer balls also could be cut out and folded in half, so friends could write him a letter that also could be placed in the casket. This provides an opportunity to "say good-bye" or anything else that was left unsaid. Writing also can be healing. Doing anything is better than the despair we all felt because there was nothing we could do. Michael's friends and brothers were going to take part in the funeral service; serving as ushers and giving readings gave them "something to do."

Photos and snapshots have become an accepted display

in funeral homes, and I watched students go to these collages and point and tell each other what they already knew about different events in Michael's life depicted there. "Hey, that was the game against Highlands. Man, we froze in that rain. Remember Michael saying that if we just acted like we were warmer than the other guys, maybe we could psyche 'em out." Then the tears welled up. I encouraged them to go ahead and cry—that it's actually good for us—and I told them what we know about the immune system and the release of endorphins in the brain. They looked to me for more information, but I turned the conversation over to them by saying, "You know, I didn't know Michael, and everyone says he was a great guy. Tell me about him." This released a flood of memories and descriptions. One boy told me that Michael taught him how to play hockey, and I asked him if he was still playing.

He said, "Yes."

"So I guess you will always have a part of Michael with you every time you play, won't you?"

He nodded, looking back at his friend in the casket.

"And no one can ever take that away from you, can they?"

He shook his head and cried. We stood there awhile without speaking. I patted his shoulder. "That's good," he said, looking up at me, then retreated to the safety of a circle of friends.

I was there that night because Michael's Uncle John was more than just one of my teachers, he had also become my friend. I had hired him right out of school, and he had become an exceptional teacher. He also is the same age as my own son. The death of his brother, Larry, had been a steep hill for John to climb, and it had given him age and wisdom he did not desire. I knew he felt like his family was doomed or plagued. So, I wanted to be there for him. Then when his sister-in-law, Michael's mother, heard I had come she hoped I would also help the children. So, I stood and waited and watched for moments to do so. I remembered that much of this work is waiting and watching and walking a careful line of respect and privacy and comfort. But I also knew that most people I had worked with said that they preferred that people say something like, "I know there are no words" than to say nothing. Everyone also agrees that "being there" is most important, but words are still our primary mode of communication. So I reviewed in my mind words and phrases that I knew to be helpful in eliciting a response, which is no easy task with teenagers.

I approached a group of boys standing in front of the casket and said, "This must seem so unreal." A couple of them turned and looked at me. Then I asked, "Were you classmates or teammates?" And they opened up. They told me things that seemed entirely irrelevant ("We were in the same class in fourth grade"), but I have learned that no sharing is meaningless and that processing is processing, no matter what the words. One of the boys said nothing and had turned back and was staring at his dead friend. He never spoke or acknowledged me. But I knew he heard the conversation with the others, and I did not try to coax him. I told the boys a little bit about shock and denial and to realize that it will take their brains awhile to take in this awful truth that Michael is dead. I told them that feeling guilty for being alive is normal, too. I asked them what they thought Michael would say to them, if he could give them some advice. One boy said he would say, "Go for it and never give up!" It was important for the silent boy to hear this. I knew to never forget that sometimes children want to die to be with their lost friend or to be relieved of life's difficulties, perceived or real.

Then I asked this grieving group what they would say to Michael if they could. A boy from Michael's neighborhood said he would want to thank him for all the time he spent working out with him playing basketball. Another said he would thank him for being such a good friend. I told them they could write these important messages to Michael, or they could tell him, even now. I saw one of these young men standing later alone at the casket, talking. We cannot measure the positive impact of this type of interaction, often until years later, but we have plenty of information about the negative impact of living with regrets for a lifetime.

Next I approached a group of girls and introduced myself as someone who worked with Michael's Uncle John in his school in New Jersey. One by one, they shook my hand telling me their first and last names. Then a girl with a beautiful smile that included braces took my hand and said with the confidence of a diplomat, "I'm Sarah." And I knew in a flash she was Michael's girlfriend, and I said so. She nodded her head and dropped it to hide her tears. I hugged her and said that I was sure she was the perfect girlfriend for Michael and that I knew she would miss him. She nodded again, so I asked, "What do you dread the most?"

Without hesitation, she said, "Sunday mornings."

I asked, "Why Sunday mornings?" And she proceeded to tell me that she and Michael always got up early on Sundays before the rest of their families and got on the Internet. Once there they would go into a chat room and talk. Whichever of them got up first found the chat room and left a message for the other. And now she dreads

Sundays because there will be no message from Michael. I could feel the longing in her story and wondered how hard it must be to accept the death of one with whom she may have shared her first kiss. I told her I would be thinking of her on Sunday mornings, and I suggested that she try her hand at writing in those early morning hours. Instead of avoiding the computer, she could use it to write about her feelings and in particular about Michael. A friend distracted her, and she was off into a conversation about clothes or something else typical of a teenage girl's conversation. It seemed to be a healthy balance that these teenagers had found moving between the horror of reality and the normalcy of wondering what to wear. I left that group wishing again for the dream I had fantasized for years, that there could be some divine exchange of messages between earth and heaven. I wished for Sarah one more message from Michael.

Wes: A High School Junior

Wes was dying of cancer, and no further treatment was recommended. He was at home, and everyone in the family was trying to live out life as normally as possible with a sword hanging over their heads. His mother was concerned that he was not "talking about it" with anyone. When I came into town after the holidays, she asked me to come over saying, "If anyone can get him to talk, you can." I reminded her that teenagers have an ability to pull inside to a place where few adults can reach, and, that if her son was not talking to family and friends, the likelihood of him talking to me was remote. I went anyway, though, because that is something we can always do—go anyway—even if we think we can do nothing to help. Showing up can make a difference.

So we sat at the kitchen table on Saturday morning with bagels and fruit and multiple cups of coffee. With this aching mother and her other children I talked about school, sports, the recent news and the weather. I used every prompt I knew to involve Wes, to no avail. At 11:45, he stood up and said he needed to go finish something on his computer. He thanked me for coming, as I was sure he had thanked other visitors. I smiled and said, "Hey, I'm thrilled you sat here with me this long." His siblings looked relieved, and everyone stood and stretched. The "chat" was obviously over and a bust!

Sue and I cleared the table, and I told her I was sorry. I gathered my keys and was at the door when one of the kids came in with the mail. The family dog bounded in, too, and headed for Wes in the den. Sue went after Puff calling to the other kids, "I told you guys to put her in the garage while Sally was here. Come get her. She stinks." I peeked in the den and saw Puff with her front paws on Wes's lap, getting the attention she desired. He looked up at me and said, "Mom won't let her in anymore when company comes."

I raised my eyebrows and asked, "Why?"

"It's her sores," he replied while scratching her ears and rubbing noses with her. "They stink," he continued, "and there's nothing more we can do to get rid of them, is there old girl?"

Since this exchange was greater than what we had during our chat at the kitchen table, I tried to keep it going. I also drew the parallel between Puff's untreatable sores and Wes's cancer. So I asked what caused the sores, and Wes explained. He gave me the history of her illnesses and what the vet had done to help. All the while, he was petting and loving this aging family dog that had become a vehicle for expression of his own illness. I asked how Puff seemed to be bearing up through all of this, and we talked about pain medications. He surmised that it probably helped, but it also made her quite lethargic. He said that he knew that she dreamed of chasing squirrels but just couldn't get the job done anymore. "We probably should have her 'put down,' but none of us can do it," he said. "She's been a member of this family since we moved here fourteen years ago. And we've been through a lot together, haven't we, old girl?"

"Hey, look what we just got, Sally," his mother said, walking into the room with the mail. "A Christmas card from your daughter. You remember them, Wes," she said, handing him the card. "Their son, Henry, was born with complications and has cerebral palsy." He struggled to stand, and we stood on either side of him. All of our eyes focused on Henry, looking grand on a bearskin rug in his birthday suit. His mom slipped her arm around Wes's waist, and he leaned on her shoulder saying, "He looks as healthy as any other baby on a bearskin rug, but I guess looks can be deceiving, can't they?"

"Yes," I said, "I saw his MRI. We don't know what the future holds." By this time, all three of us were unsuccessfully choking back tears.

"Poor little guy," Wes said, "he probably has a rough road ahead of him."

"Yes, I think you're right, but I don't think we could love him any more than we do. He is so special to us," I answered.

"Then he's lucky to have the family he has, isn't he?" Wes concluded as he sat back down at his computer.

"Well, we think we are the ones who are lucky."

Wes looked over at his mother who was smiling that same message right at him.

Sue and I stood by my car, while she thanked me for being there. I told her I gained more than I gave. I learned again that day to listen to everything people say, regardless of the subject. Sometimes it's direct. Sometimes it isn't. Sometimes it's through their own story. Sometimes it's through the story of their dog, or their soccer team or their looming science test. But it is only when they feel safe and valued that they will share themselves with you. I keep that Christmas card of Henry to remind me of this important lesson.

Kathy: A Parent

The phone rang at 6:15 A.M. On a school day, that usually meant something was wrong at school: The boiler's down, there's a leak, someone needs help. On this morning something was very wrong. A parent was dead. I mentally indexed the name and realized her children were in the primary grades. An instantaneous picture of her came to mind. I had last seen her teaching the aerobics/kick boxing club after school three days earlier: tiny, cute, energetic, involved. The image of her dead did not compute, and the next piece of information didn't either: She had died of a self-inflicted gunshot wound. My heart sank momentarily, but I quickly mobilized myself, grabbed my keys and headed for the school. As a principal, I wanted to get a memo out to the faculty informing them and directing them in the best, most sensitive way to handle this tragedy. I knew what I needed to do this day and wondered how many school principals know, too. My guess was not many. I wouldn't have known either had I not been doing this grief work for many years. There were no courses in either of my graduate programs that prepared me, or other people studying school administration, for handling death in school.

There were only a couple of cars in the parking lot when I arrived. I hurried into the office, turned on the computer, and was writing furiously when the chief of police arrived to inform me. I raised my hand as though to stop him and said, "Don't tell me anything, Rich, because I am writing a memo saying 'all we know at this time is that this mother of two of our students died last night in an accident in her home. If anyone asks for more details or says what they have heard, we need to say that nothing else has been confirmed.' That is what happened, isn't it?" He nodded, and I continued, "So, I can say this is all we know at this time, and I will be telling the truth." He gave me a little smile as he said, "Sure." But his eyes betrayed his smile with the pained expression of having to be the bearer of such tragic news. Then we sat in my office with a cup of coffee and ached for this little family as he told me the details. She shot herself in the heart. He told me her husband, Ken, was terribly distraught. He had been at work when she died, and the kids had spent the night at their grandparents' house and didn't even know yet.

After the students arrived and school was underway, I called the father's sister-in-law, whose daughter was also in our school and a close cousin to the children, who did not

yet know their mother was dead. I asked her if she thought
her brother-in-law would want me to come over to the
house to talk to the children and assured her I would be
happy to do so. She told me how devastated they all were
and that Ken had called a local counseling agency to send
someone over to "tell" the children, because he didn't want
to say the wrong thing. He wanted to protect them, to spare
them this pain, she said, and I remembered wanting to do
the same for my children when their father died. So now, I
pleaded with her to call Ken and ask him if he would let me
"tell" the children, but before she could answer, I said,
"Never mind, I need to call him myself." And did so.

The first question he asked me was, "Why would you
want to do that?" I told him that he probably did not know
that I do work in the area of grief and loss and that, while
no one wants to deal with such painful situations, I, at least,
had experience. I also told him that I would gladly and willingly do it for him and the kids, especially because I am
someone they know, someone they trust. He agreed, and I
hurried out to my car. As I adjusted the rearview mirror, I
realized that I had not put on any makeup and my hair was
just as it had shook out after my shower. As I moved my
hand in a futile attempt to spruce up a little, I knew that no
one would notice, not on this day, not in that house. My
going there was what mattered. My desire to help, my comfort, my presence were what would make a difference. My
appearance was irrelevant.

As I came to the door, Kimberly saw me and squealed,
"Dr. Downham! Hey, Dad, Dr. Downham is here. What
are you doing here?" Now, children know far more than we
adults remember that we knew, too, when we were young.
They knew their dad was home early. They knew he was

upset. They knew their grandmother was crying. They knew their aunt and cousin were not in school. They knew the school principal doesn't make house calls. They could feel the tension in the air. They knew something was wrong with this day. They also knew their mother was fragile and had not been "feeling well" for weeks. So, I put my arm around her shoulders and said, "I have something I want to tell you. Where is your brother?" She ran off to find him, and I hugged the grandmother, whom I had only met once before.

"Thank God you're here," she whispered and let me hold her while she began to sob.

"I'm so glad I am here today, so I could come," I replied, then asked her if she had an egg. She pulled back to see if she had heard me correctly and headed for her refrigerator. By this time the children were back in the living room and I suggested that we sit on the floor. With their father, grandparents, aunts and uncles in the chairs around us, I said, "I want to tell you a story and you are going to help me."

I opened my hand and showed them the egg and said, "Now, I don't have to tell you that this is an egg, but I do want you to tell me what you know about it." Once again the memory of doing this exact same exercise with my daughter, Tamara, was a powerful presence. I allowed myself to reach back into that experience and re-feel the pain, because I know there is connection between all of our painful losses that creates a closeness between us, even when we are not close. It is what gave me the credibility to walk into a place where others would hesitate to go. It is what allows me to touch another's broken heart and bring comfort. It made me a part of the family that day, to feel with them, ache with them, cry with them. This is empathy.

Sympathy does not have this same power. I could have come just to teach them what I know about grief, but that doesn't have much power either. I could have waited until I could bring food or send flowers, the way I had been taught, but what they needed was more than anything physical could salve.

When the questions were answered, we had asserted that the purpose of the eggshell was to protect the tender, inner good parts of the egg. Then I said, "We are kind of like this egg. We have a shell, too." Then I asked them what our shells are like. They went through the list of hair, skin and bones. I told them that our shell protects the fragile part of us, the best part of us. "And even though some people act like the shell is the best part, I'll bet you know that the best part is what is in our hearts, don't you?"

They said, "Yes."

Then I led them into a discussion about the ways our "shells" get sick and went through the list of diseases I was fairly certain they knew. "So when we die we don't need these shells anymore, do we?" I asked.

They said, "No," and went on to tell me that they believed that the good part goes to heaven. I breathed a sigh of relief that they had offered this information, because I then said, "The reason I came to talk to you today and tell you this story is because your mommy died last night."

They whirled around to their father and saw his tears and began clamoring for information. I asked their dad to sit with us, and he got down on the floor and embraced his children, and I began to inform them in a far gentler voice that Mommy had a sickness that affected her brain and she was not able to think clearly. I told them that sometimes a sickness in our brain causes people to hurt themselves and not do the right or safe thing. But the most important thing I told them on that floor was that their mother loved them and did not want to leave them. I also told them that she was proud of them and would never want to hurt them. But her hurt, her pain, her sickness was what caused her to hurt herself.

Then Kimberly asked, "How did she die?"

Her father replied, "She shot herself," and they both cried and said, "No, oh no."

Earlier when I first came to the house, Ken had asked me if there was any way we could spare the children from knowing how their mother died, and as I hugged this aching dad, I said, "No, there really is not. I wish there were, but there just isn't. It has been on the police radio and people will know, and, unfortunately, when people know they talk. I know you would never want them to hear it from someone else, especially a kid at school, so I think it is better to deal with it up front and now. This will be the hardest part, and if you can do it today, I promise you it will get easier the next time you have to say it. Don't forget that the kids know more than you think. They know all about their mother's struggle and her sickness, even if it was never named or discussed. So we want them to hear this in a way that they can accept and yet not feel responsible, because kids will take it on themselves if they have to guess or wonder what really happened. I will help you. We'll do it together."

By the time his daughter asked him how her mother died, Ken had the strength to tell her. He shared this difficult information with a minimum of details, and we all agreed that telling people that she died in an accident was adequate. Because of his honesty, the children asked him a number of questions. They sat together on the floor talking and crying, until no one spoke, and I said, "How about a drink of water?" Everyone stood up and seemed grateful for something normal to do. Ken's mother offered coffee, and we sat in the living room in that shock-induced malaise and marveled that the children went off to play. I stayed a while knowing full well that the children would have more to ask, and in ten minutes they were back. I left late morning and went back to the school to prepare everyone for a similar discussion with the first- and third-grade classes and the egg.

In the classroom discussions, I began by telling the children that their classmate's mother had died, and then I asked how many children had experienced the death of someone in their family. The expected number of grandparent deaths was reported, along with a few others. No one's mother, however, had died. We talked about how everything living dies and went through flowers dying, trees dying and even pets dying. Then I asked them what happens to a person when they die. Some children talked about heaven and God, and, of course, one student, as is typical, talked about everyone getting buried in the ground and having worms crawl out our noses. I minimized the comment with some reference to caskets and graves today preventing those circumstances but recalled the kid in my own third-grade class who would have made the same comment. Then I pulled out my egg.

The discussion that followed emphasized for these very young children that when we die, we no longer see or hear or feel anything. This is a difficult concept for children, and without this understanding children have been known to have nightmares and fears that stay with them for years. So we spent some time talking about what is reality and then generating ideas about what we could do to help. I asked the children if it made a difference how a person dies or that, in fact, the person was dead. I asked them if they thought it would help their classmates feel better if they talked about the way their mom died or if there was something else they could say that would be comforting. They all agreed that finding kind and helpful things to say would be best, and we began brainstorming some words and phrases. The younger children drew pictures, and the older ones wrote letters of condolence to be given to their classmates. These often are priceless gems that families keep for generations. It is important to preview them, however, for any that would be insensitive or hurtful. For instance, one first-grader drew a picture of a woman in a casket and wrote the word "Ded" three times at the bottom of the page. That one did not make the cut. I took these gifts to the family after school and had a little chat with the children about funeral homes and caskets and ceremonies. I went home around 6:00 P.M. It was a long day. Grief work takes time, but it is always time well spent.

At the funeral home Bucky, the six-year-old, was telling everyone with confidence, "I know Mommy looks like she is sleeping, but she isn't there. That's just her shell, kind of like an eggshell. The best part of her has gone to heaven."

The work of grieving, however, comes long after the funeral ceremonies are over and everyone else gets back to their normal lives. Ken had both insight and experience enough to know that they would need help and sought out a therapist. He came to school to check in with me often and to apprise me of their progress. In May, on the Friday before Mother's Day our school has a plant sale, so children can purchase flowers inexpensively for their moms. Ken took the day off from work and came to school. He told his kids that they would do this for Mom. I will always remember him standing behind a table in the lobby of the school with a money apron on, helping other people's children buy flowers for their mothers. His children came to help after school, and Kimberly told me, as she slipped a plant into a brown paper bag for a kindergartner, that this is how they were celebrating Mother's Day. By connecting this activity with the memory of their mom they were beginning the healing that would take place again on every Mother's Day for a long time to come. There are some losses that we live with for a lifetime.

Mandy: A High School Senior

This call came from a teacher in the high school from which Amanda had just graduated. It was summer vacation now, with no students or teachers at the school, but this teacher knew the kids would need something more. We discussed some possibilities, and then I called the principal and told him about our ideas. He said we were welcome to use the cafeteria for a gathering, so the teacher "put out the word." I continue to be amazed at how quickly people share information when there has been a death or tragedy, and this proved so again in this suburban community. The next day I received a call from the local newspaper saying they had heard I was leading a grief session for Mandy's friends the next evening and wanted to know some lead information about what would take place. I told him. Then I said, "If you send a reporter, please convey my earnest desire for her to sit in the audience and be a part of the evening, rather than sit in the back or along a side wall, with a pad and pencil writing." I also said no photographers. By this time, I had spoken with a number of teachers, who had been quite upset with the media presence at the memorial service in the gym and the way photographers were taking pictures of students in the throes of their grief.

Amanda's death was tragically sensational. In this Midwestern city close to Chicago, railroad crossings are plentiful. When the guard arms are down, no cars should cross. In reality, some do. In this situation, she did. There were two trains. She could see the first one waiting at the crossing, going nowhere. She was late for a beauty appointment.

Friends were coming into town for the weekend, and she was in a hurry. A couple of cars ahead of her drove around the guard arms and went on their way. So she crossed the tracks. What she could not see was the train coming from the opposite direction, obscured by a building on her right. Neither she nor the engineer of the second train saw each other until she drove into his path.

We set the chairs in a horseshoe arrangement in the cafeteria with only three or four rows of seats and an aisle in the middle. I asked the custodian if he could put a couple of stacks of chairs in the back of the room, in case I needed them. When a few teachers came, they suggested we set up some more chairs, but I said, "Let's wait." If the students in this high school were like all other teenagers I had met, they would come in and sit in the back rows first. Then as others arrived, they would have to take the seats closer to the front. So, I wanted to wait until all of the seats were taken, then I could signal the custodian to set up more. The closeness of the gathering is important, and when the front rows are empty there is a message of "some are missing" that I did not want. I prepared a packet of information about grief and had it on a table. The only other equipment I had was an overhead projector.

As people entered the room, I watched these teenagers find each other and form little groups. They put their arms around each other briefly, then either put their hands deep in their pockets or crossed them in front of their chests, as though holding in their fragile guts. They had suffered the death of another classmate earlier in the year; Amity died of a brain tumor.

No one sat down. I was surprised at how many adults were there: teachers, parents, family friends. A soft-spoken, diminutive woman came up to me, with her husband lingering a few steps behind, and said, "I'm Mandy's mother." I held her hands in both of mine, wanting to hug her, but I realize that we walk a fine line in this teaching/comforting role. So I resisted the urge. There we were relating to each other regarding one of the most intimate and personal events of their lives, yet we were strangers.

Those of us who do this work are not necessarily personal friends, ministers or counselors. We are teachers of grief, educators sharing ideas for coping and directions for comfort. While the connection to each other is vital, some distance is important for the teaching to be heard. Emotion distracts us from what is going on around us. Powerful emotion can blot it all out. Navigating that precarious line between emotion and reason, heart and brain, is an ongoing struggle for balance. Touching someone whose grief is new is like touching the roof of a canvas tent in the rain and watching the water come through immediately.

I thanked Mandy's parents for coming and told them how much it would mean to her friends that they were there.

Then I moved around the room and gently asked everyone to find a seat. I introduced myself and told them how sorry I was that Mandy had died and they had lost their friend. Then I told them that I wanted to talk to them about their grief. I explained that grief is a natural response to loss. Everyone grieves. How we grieve depends on what society and family mores and individuals allow. I told them that this evening was set aside for them to grieve and that it was my hope that they would leave knowing a little more about dealing with grief when it occurs over time. Then I told them my story. I glanced at the clock to remind myself to keep this part brief, but the story is important, because it gives me credibility. I especially picked parts of my story that would relate more closely to their lives and circumstances, like how young my first husband was when he died. I told them how difficult it was to think of his strong, handsome body dead. I knew her best friends were there. She and her girlfriends likely spent a lot of time focusing on their appearances. Clothes, body shapes, attractiveness of hair and nails occupy much of teenage girls' conversations and activities. She was hurrying to a beauty shop appointment when she was killed. I also knew her male friends were there, and they certainly were not attracted only to her bright mind and personality. All teaching should relate to the student's life and circumstances, whenever possible. The probability of retention of information increases dramatically.

I turned on the overhead projector and wrote down the name Elisabeth Kubler-Ross and asked if anyone had heard of her. Then I told them that she was a physician who worked with terminally ill people and their families. Her first book on this topic was called *On Death and Dying*. In it, she wrote her observations about the similarities in the patterns of her patients' reactions to dying. Then with an enlightening new honesty, she also reported that her patients' families exhibited strikingly similar reactions. With this work, she began a new discussion about how we respond to loss and death, in what she called "stages of grief." Then I picked up the overhead marker and wrote the word "anger." Some of the guys who were slumped in their chairs with their baseball caps pulled low over their eyes looked up. Then I gave a brief description of this natural reaction to loss and shared with them Kubler-Ross's other stages of denial, bargaining, depression and acceptance. I used myself as an example. I interjected a little self-effacing humor here to demonstrate that it is okay to laugh in the middle of grief. Then I said, "We will come back to this, but now let's talk about Mandy." The room held its breath.

I put a new transparency on the overhead and said, "I did not know Mandy, but everything I have heard about her leads me to believe she was quite special. So, I want you to tell me about her. The best way to do this is for you to describe her in single words or short phrases. So, let's begin."

Now, every time I do this there is usually silence, for a variety of reasons. No one wants to go first. No one wants to appear foolish. Some people are afraid they will cry if they try to speak. So, I usually say something in a light-hearted manner like, "This is the audience participation part of the program, and it goes like this: I ask a question and you answer it. Get it? Okay, now let's start again. How would you describe Mandy?" When I did this everyone relaxed and even chuckled a little bit.

Then I heard a small voice say, "Impatient!" I looked for the source of the answer and it was Carol, Mandy's mom. I smiled at her bravery and said, "I'll bet that is pretty closely tied to that anger stage we were talking about a few moments ago, isn't it?" She nodded her head affirmatively. This was a great first response, and it isn't always so. But, whatever the first response is, it must be reinforced positively so others will feel freer to participate.

I looked at another section of the audience and said, "Tell me what she looked like." Words like "perky," "brunette," "beautiful smile," started off the list, and the discussion was off and running. Then deeper feelings were expressed in phrases like: "thoughtful," "sexy," "enthusiastic." Next, I asked them to list what they will miss the most, and they discussed how she was always helping someone, how much she loved flowers, how she organized everyone and "made us do things together." One young man asked how to deal with all that was left unsaid, undone. I guessed that this might have been a "special" friend. I could tell by his regret that there was an opportunity missed, something put off that he now could not do. So I suggested that he write Mandy a letter or write about her. I even thought it might be helpful to mail it, perhaps, even address the envelope to her in care of her family.

As this discussion continued, I wrote everything on the overhead projector that I had focused on an empty wall of the cafeteria. This made the writing bigger than it would have been if limited to a screen. So, on the wall in front of them emerged a description of this beautiful friend and classmate. It was my hope that this would reconnect them with the times when they came into this room just to eat lunch together, never dreaming that they would come here to discuss ways to live out their lives after her death.

When the Mandy List was full, we turned our attention

back to our list of stages of grief. I explained that they are
not like stages in the growth of a seed that begin with planting the seed in soil and watching the stages of gestation.
"Grief is far less predictable," I told them. "One day you
may be angry and not want to talk about it and just act like
a grouch. The next day, or five minutes later, you may feel
an overwhelming sense of longing and want to talk about
everything you did together. Then you may want to forget it
ever happened, go to bed and wake up in the morning,
hopefully, to find it was all a bad dream. But, experiencing
anger one day and something else the next does not mean
you are finished with anger. There are no steps that form a
sequence that everyone should follow, but all of these
responses are common to each of us who are grieving. So
let's list them and acknowledge them, and they will have far
less power over us."

We listed all of the emotions they had experienced since
her death. Then I asked them to tell me the things they had
thought of that they knew would not happen, big and small,
because she was gone. One girl said, "She was the only
friend I had who would paint my toenails." And I explained
that it is these day-to-day things that make up our grief and
bring up those powerful feelings we had just listed. I suggested that they needed to be patient with each other when
someone else is not where they are in this process and to be
understanding with each other as they work this through on
different timetables.

Next, I asked them what they could "do." Doing is important in this grief work and finding what to do is not easy. So,
we brainstormed some ideas. Some of her friends already
had planted a tree with her favorite flowers, daisies, around
it in her front yard. They discussed things like scholarships

and memorial awards, and getting daisy tattoos. But the best idea came, interestingly, from a farmer nearby. He owned a small barn on the outskirts of his land that was across the street from the school. For years kids had painted graffiti on it and, when caught, were required to pay to clean it off and personally repaint the barn. After enough of this, the farmer decided to donate his barn's "billboarding" qualities to the students, so they could write supportive slogans on it for athletic games and important school events. Now, it had become a memorial site, too. So, both the talented and lesser-skilled students could all play a part. They honored Amity's life there also, and two angels eventually were painted with words of love and friendship written around them. This may have been some of the most positive, therapeutic "doing" these students would experience.

By this time an hour and a half had passed, and I knew that a saturation point had been reached. I asked for questions and found myself wondering where the reporter was sitting. Her presence was not obvious, and I was silently grateful that she had joined the group. She spoke later to some of the kids and their parents, and her article is in Part IV, Section A. In Part IV, Section E is a piece that Mandy Jackson's friend Jason wrote about her after she died.

Tom: A First-Grader

His mother hates windy weather. She grew up on the East Coast and still is not accustomed to the unexpected gusts of power that accompany springtime weather in the Midwest.

This Sunday, she watched the trees in the yard wrestle to hold
their places as she answered the phone. A mother from Little
League was calling to ask a favor. Mary Ellen agreed to take
her place driving to the game, but thought about how much
she would hate to drive the van out on the windy country
roads to Mulberry Park, where the game was being played.
She wished Mike could do it, but he was taking their second
son, Dan, to Purdue University to sign up for summer basketball camp and would have to arrive separately. She hustled
up the other two boys, and they piled in the van to pick up a
couple of teammates on their way to the game. She was glad
Tom, her youngest, could run around and play in the park
while the game was going on. He always needed to run off
some steam. He was so antsy earlier in the morning in church
that she made him sit on her lap to hold him still. Matt, the
oldest brother, was chatting with his buddies and seemed
oblivious to the way the van was buffeted about by the wind.

"I'm not sure if the game is going to take place at all in
this wind," she said over her right shoulder to the boys in
the seat behind her. But they seemed unaffected by it all.
She looked for Mike's car as they arrived at the park, and
wondered why they always seem to have two cars at the
same events. The players were warming up on the field.
Tom found a friend, and together they ran off to play on the
swings and slides nearby. She stood by the car with a sense
of dread and kept an eye out for Mike and Dan. When she
saw them drive into the parking lot, she relaxed a little and
settled into her seat on the bleachers. The chatter with the
other parents included a discussion of how many innings
they would have to play before canceling the game.
Everyone kept watch on the clouds. The wind blew up
swirls of dirt on the infield, and by the third inning the

pitcher's hat blew off his head and they had to stop the game momentarily. Mary Ellen wished they would call it off completely, but play resumed.

Then the storm hit.

Everyone scattered like ants on a Raid commercial, grabbing jackets as they ran for their cars or the picnic shelter. The roar of the wind prevented everyone from hearing what the person next to them was saying, but Mike had no trouble understanding the word Mary Ellen's mouth formed. "Tom." And she pointed beyond the picnic shelter to the area where the boys were playing moments ago on a self-propelled merry-go-round. They both ran by other people calling his name, their screams nearly muted by the din and screech of the storm. Twisterlike swirls scorched dust and sand in their eyes and prevented them from seeing the tree that fell on the merry-go-round, pinning both boys underneath heavy limbs.

Mike is a physician, and Mary Ellen was an experienced nurse. They were trained to remove all emotion in emergencies, but surely no instructor in their medical training could have given any wisdom for handling this emergency. Not for their own son. Their Tom. But they did it. Without consultation, Mike ran to Tom and Mary Ellen to Jacob. How they broke through branches and leaves with the wind still ripping at their clothes cannot be explained. How Mike removed a huge branch off of Tom that was still attached to the tree was a miraculous feat that he barely remembers. Jacob had been thrown free. Mary Ellen rolled his head to one side and began to clear his mouth to start CPR. He had vomited. She cleared the pathway again and continued giving the lifesaving breaths she knew could save him until the EMT arrived. With no concept of time or space she prayed not to vomit herself. Then, after what seemed an eternity, huge strong arms lifted her off the ground, away from Jacob and began carrying her toward the shelter. She struggled to free herself and get to Mike and Tom. She needed to be with them, not dragged off to the shelter, but the med-techs were putting Tom on a stretcher. Now there was nothing to do. No running. No scrambling to find him. No working to save him. No chance to hold him one more time. To protect him. For a parent and a nurse there isn't anything worse than realizing there is nothing you can do. Someone put a blanket around her and held onto her shaking body. The cold aftermath of shock had set in. She heard the voices around her, trying to reassure her, telling her "everything will be okay." But she knew what she knew and no words could reach her. The smell of Jacob's vomit would be in her mind and nasal passages for days and weeks and even in dark dreams over the years.

Mike knew, too. Tom still had a pulse when Mike freed him from the limbs that crushed him, but he wasn't breathing. Mike administered CPR and, in that position, could see the damage to Tom's skull. He rode to the hospital in the ambulance with this patient/child he could not save. When the greater pain of a father's love and fear came to the fore, he pushed it down, reminding himself that the best father he could be for Tom was to be doctor first and father second. Two of the top neurosurgeons in the area were waiting for him in the ER. They wanted to save Tom, too, but Mike could tell when they finished examining him that surgery was not going to help. They were friends, these three physicians. They went to conferences together, golfed together, helped each other when called. Now they stood together in a conference room next to the ER and knew there was nothing any of them could do.

Someone drove Mary Ellen and Matt and Dan to the hospital. She remembered asking them to pray as they raced across town. The storm had passed. The nothingness inside of her was mirrored by the empty aftermath of the wind. She tried to prevent her mind from going back to the internal premonitions and intuitions she had earlier in the day. She began the destructive parent pattern of blaming herself for not being all-powerful or not being all-knowing or, at least, not acting on her motherly intuition that had said, "Don't go to this game. It's too windy. A storm is brewing." She also knew that if she kept her family home every time the wind blew, they would not go out at all in the springtime and that was ridiculous. But those are the things a parent in shock thinks about. Other voices barely can be heard. Parental instinct is a powerful thing.

The whole family was together for the last time at the hospital when they stood around Tom's body. His little hands still had traces of the dirt that was so quintessentially Tom after play.

What can be said? What advice can be given? What fool would dare to contribute the thought that someday they would be "over it"? Who, with what gall, would suggest that they would need to find closure? What does that mean anyway? Forgetting it? Having no memory of it? Not being able to close your eyes and see it all and smell the vomit and feel the panic? Is anyone thick enough to think that is possible? If not, then why do people suggest it or imply it, even years later? If "getting over it" is an unrealistic expectation, why do people talk about it as though that is something we can expect? "Shouldn't you be over it by now?" is the most common horrible thing grieving people are asked to their faces. What does that mean? Will the day actually come when they take a deep breath and sigh and say that it wasn't so bad after all? *Come on!!*

Nine years later, Mike and Mary Ellen still go to the ballgames. Matt graduated from Indiana University last year, and Dan is a junior there. They are both terrific athletes and remarkable young men. Tom would have been, too. Is it difficult to go to the games and watch Tom's classmates and wonder what position Tom would have played, had he lived, or which of the cute girls would have been his girlfriend? Yes, of course it is difficult. But they know the alternative is worse. To withdraw, to disconnect is another kind of death. To remember keeps them "put together" as a family. They always say when asked in casual conversation by strangers, "We have three boys."

They took the monetary gifts from the community to build a Little League field in their hometown in Tom's memory. People donated time, energy and expertise. It was important to Mike and Mary Ellen that the field be lighted. That way the kids could play at night. The game could always go on! It is full of life every spring when the anniversary of Tom's death comes around. His older brother Matt designed the monument at the entrance. It is a climbing rock for children to play on while their brothers and sisters are inside the field, playing ball. One side is an incline, the other steps. The top is flattened to allow a couple of kids to stand up like they are "king of the hill" or sit on it and watch the game. The memorial plaque in Tom's honor is on one side, down near the ground. Some of the kids who play on it don't know who Tom Skehan is, but the parents who come there to watch their kids play know. The story is told

over and over again in the bleachers there. It is a living
memorial. Tom would have loved playing there.

At home, Mary Ellen eventually turned Tom's room into
a studio where she took up flower arranging and other artis-
tic endeavors. That has allowed her to go in there and "do"
something. There is nothing more empty for a parent than
the room of a child who is gone. She kept his pictures and
drawings and things around, so it is still Tom's room. Doing
something helps. Being able to start a project and finish it
helps, because there is so little we can "do" in the aftermath
of such a great loss. They talk about Tom without idealizing
him. That keeps him "real" in their memories.

Jerry Downham, my brother-in-law, built their new
house, and we met them at the Downham Custom Homes
Christmas party. Jerry told me about Tom's baseball field.
We both wiped away tears in a corner as we remembered
Bob, his brother and my first husband, who lived about
twenty years longer than their Tommy but left just as big a
hole in our lives. That kind of similarity can be comforting
if we are brave enough to share it with each other. Mary
Ellen and Mike have become good friends with Will and
me. I was honored that they would tell me their story. They
said they were honored to have Tom in my book. This kind
of friendship is golden. It is mourning and dancing.

Ian's Near-Death

When Director Dave Wright called me at home one summer morning I thought he sounded like he had a cold, until
he said, "There's been an accident." As a member of the

board of directors of this extraordinary YMCA camp
named for the Native American Chief Tecumseh, I hoped
the accident was not in the newly opened swimming pool.
My fears, however, were confirmed when David said,
"We hope and pray the child lives, Sally, and that we've had
just a near-drowning."

As a special after-dinner treat for their campers, the
counselors in the boys' cabins let their thirteen-year-old
charges play "sharks and minnows" in the pool. The job of
the many minnows is to catch, by tagging, the elusive shark,
who we will call Ian, before he reached the opposite side of
the pool. Ian was a strong swimmer and could go from one
side of the pool to the other underwater with ease and made
a perfect shark. After crossing the pool underwater for
three previous rounds, he came to the surface safely. The
guys there cheered, likely realizing they could never catch
him. After surfacing briefly he dropped down under the
water, almost like he was relieved he had won. However, he
did not come back up. Within seconds the kids and the lifeguard were saying, "Where is he? What's he doing down
there?" And the lifeguard dove to find out. In the few seconds it took to bring Ian to the surface, he was already blue.
The lifeguard shouted to two staff members nearby to call
911 and help him. Fortunately, the two staff members
nearby were training to become emergency medical techni-
cians. They administered CPR until the ambulance arrived,
but the early reports were grim.

I arrived at the camp and Dave asked me if I would meet
first with the staff of Ian's cabin-mates. I said, "Of course,"
but I was not prepared for what I found in the living room
of Dave and Beth's home on campus. Everyone was crying.
The despair was palpable. The regret and responsibility

these people felt were expressed in sentences that began with words like, "If only I would have . . ." and "I should have . . ." and "Why didn't we . . . ?"

When an accident happens in a school or a camp like this one, those of us in charge are usually keenly aware that the parents have put their children in our care, believing they will be safe. It is difficult, at best, not to blame ourselves or someone else. So this group seemed inconsolable. I spoke to them about accidents and how they happen, even with the closest, most conscientious supervision available, and how they cannot always be prevented. I reminded them of the definition of "accident." I had them retell the story over again to show them what I already knew. They, in fact, had saved Ian's life. But they didn't see it that way. They blamed themselves for not being omnipotent or, at least, omniscient. So, we talked about shock and trauma and guilt and regret —all of which are normal grief reactions. Then we talked about ways to help each other, ways to dialogue, ways to help the children process this event. Their willingness to care for each other and to help the kids was extraordinary.

The phone rang and it was the hospital. This report was even more grim than the first. Ian was in a coma, clinging precariously to life. Dave already had sent Ian's sister, who was a counselor at camp, to the hospital with another staff member. He was leaving to go there himself, once he felt certain that the staff-in-charge had all of the resources they needed to carry on.

Next I turned my attention to the cabin of boys and their counselors, who were with Ian in the pool. I basically said all of the same things I had just said in the past hour with a slightly different spin, because I know that when people are in shock it is difficult to hear, pay attention and hold onto

information. They said very little, but sat slumped in the
chairs and couches, hiding under baseball hats and looking
at their shoes. So, I decided to have them do a writing exercise. As soon as I said, "I want you to write a letter," I realized that I had not thought through "to whom" they should
write it. If Ian died, letters from these boys to his parents
will be cherished gifts for their broken hearts. But if he
lived, shouldn't the letters be addressed to Ian, so when he
gained strength he could read them and be encouraged by
his friends? And I made a split-second decision to go with
the latter, and only when I reflected back on it did I realize
why that was the best choice. Letters written to Ian were
statements of faith and hope, and that is what both Ian and
his parents needed. So, we talked for a few minutes about
what they could say, and I wrote their ideas on a large piece
of paper that I taped on the back of a dining room chair, so
all of them could see it. Posterboard or a flip-chart would
have been nice, but in an emergency we use whatever we
can find.

When we were finished, it was time for the next camp
class. So, I asked if anyone wanted to go. About half of the
group did so. With the remaining boys, I asked them what
other losses they had experienced or what other situations
they knew of that were similar. I figured this group had
stayed because they needed more time and, possibly, may
have wanted to talk. To stimulate conversation, I used
prompts, like "Have you ever known anyone who
drowned?" and "Has anyone in your family died?" I knew
to stay away from the phrase, "What are you feeling?" By
asking about similarities and other situations, the boys
could speak freely, expressing anger or frustration or
regrets that are one step removed from their own feelings.

This hour passed quickly, and soon it was lunchtime. The boys seemed to have somewhat lighter spirits as we walked to the dining hall. Before I left them I said, "I'll meet anyone that wants to talk further right here after lunch," fairly certain no one would come. I was ready to go home. I had picked strawberries the day before and hoped to make the jam before too much time passed. And I felt a sense of closure with this initial interaction. Well, I was wrong.

After lunch, two of the boys returned to me. I asked them if they wanted to take a walk, and off we went. As we walked through the woods and around activity sites, the boys chattered about camp, sports, building fires, etc. My quickly ripening strawberries, sitting in my hot garage, kept creeping into my mind. I made myself refocus when we came to the lake. The boys began throwing pebbles into the water, and I joined them skipping a few rocks. When they had run out of things to say, it seemed our walk was over. But, when I turned to head back to the main campus, one of the boys sat down. Josh continued skipping rocks like it was an assignment I had given him, and I sat next to Paul who was doodling in the pebbles. We just sat there. I threw a few more stones in the water and, without preamble, Paul said, "I killed him, you know." I was so shocked that he spoke, I was uncertain that I had heard him correctly.

I said, "What?"

He said, "I killed Ian," and nodded his head affirmatively, as though confirming his confession.

I measured my words with care, knowing that I should not refute his statement or make any judgment that would shut him back up again.

"Tell me about it," I said, while continuing to look out at

the water, fearing that if I looked at him I would spook him. I threw a couple more rocks and waited.

He proceeded to tell me "what happened" the night before in the pool. It seems that Paul was nearly as strong as Ian and could also swim easily under water. So while Ian was trying to escape the attacking minnows, Paul was waiting for him. When Ian came close to the finish line, Paul dove down to take his arm and bring him to the surface. And Paul's fear, which in his guilt fantasy had become a certainty, was he thought he had "hooked" Ian around the throat. But Ian came to the surface and was fine. They played a number of more rounds before the accident, but when the lifeguard brought Ian to the surface, already turning blue, Paul was beside himself and was afraid to tell anyone his fear of being responsible.

It took quite a while to get this whole story straight. I asked simple questions, keeping my voice free of emotion and trying just to sound curious. I asked him to go through the events of the game over and over again, feigning a lack of understanding, but in reality wanting him to hear himself . . . wanting him to have it sink in that if he had hooked Ian around the neck to the point of injury, Ian could not have played the game for another twenty minutes. "Could he have?" I repeated.

"No," Paul was finally able to say, "I guess not."

"So, are you responsible?" I asked.

"No, but it seemed like it must have been someone's fault, and I sure didn't want it to be mine. Ian's my friend, and I'm really scared he is going to die," he sobbed.

I assured him that was everyone's fear. I scooted a little closer, and we continued to sit there for a while.

"Would you like to rewrite your letter to Ian?" I finally asked.

Paul turned and looked at me, for the first time since he had sat down, and said, "Yes."

As we walked down the road to camp, Josh, who had been with us listening to the whole exchange, gave his friend Paul a light punch in the upper arm. We stopped by Dave's house so Paul could rewrite his letter. Then they walked me to my car, and I headed home to make strawberry jam. Around eight o'clock that evening, when I was up to my ears in jam jars and exhausted, I realized what had happened that I must never forget. Kids will take more responsibility on themselves than is warranted when accidents happen or losses occur. They will blame themselves for not seeing it coming or for not knowing how to prevent it or for something they did that might have made it happen and wasn't related at all. And I realized that if I had gone home at lunchtime, Paul might have carried this horrific burden with him for the rest of his life, and who knows how that could affect a person if it is kept inside? Giving kids a safe space where they can share their fears, anger and hurt is the name of this game.

The best part of this story is that Ian survived, though it took a year or more for him to recover. It turned out to be an accident with a happy ending, but in the middle of such an event, not knowing the outcome, the grief is as powerful as in any other loss and must be processed. Ian's parents were grateful to the camp for the quick response that saved their son, and, to the delight of all of his friends, Ian returned to camp the following year.

Emily: A First-Grader's Battle with Neuroblastoma

When Carolyn Small visited our home, only weeks before her death, she insisted on helping me write this book. Hearing her voice on a tape we made that week proved her right, and she would love that. She did, indeed, help me write this book. The beautiful account she gave on that tape recording was that of the life of a child neither of us knew, Emily Rice. This little girl was a formidable force, much like Carolyn Small. They also shared a common life's passion: their school.

The key relationship between Emily and her school was, of course, her teacher. Kathy Quinn is a first-grade teacher, and she took Emily's first-grade education quite seriously. She videotaped her class, gave Emily regular assignments, went to the hospital to check her work, and provided on-site instruction when necessary. She also went and sat in a quiet space with her student, telling her stories and reading to her. While Emily was at Sloan-Kettering in New York City, Kathy would have to take the train from Waldwick, New Jersey, into Manhattan or brave the New York City traffic and drive. The hospital was not just down the street.

Emily loved having the responsibility of doing her work, and, even more, she loved feeling included with her class. Some of the last pictures she drew were of her and her friends at school. Her art work was happy and hopeful always. In the last weeks of her life, she moved the sun from one side of the page to the other and began drawing herself as an angel. Kathy says of Emily, "She was the finest teacher I have ever had. She changed my life and my attitude, and

I will never be the same because of her. It was a privilege to be her teacher."

Carolyn Small became the principal of Traphagen Elementary School two years after Emily died. When she met Emily's mom, Cyndie Rice, and her new baby girl named Hope, there was an instant bond. When Carolyn heard the story of Emily's life and death, she began the project of establishing a memorial for Emily. Today the Emily Rice Memorial Library is a tribute to both Emily and Carolyn. The memorial plaque by the door of the library is accompanied by Emily's drawings of her family and her friends.

The testimony of this brief, beautiful life is captured in the eulogy given by Emily's mother.

Emily's Eulogy

There are so many things that parents think about when they lose a child, particularly when that loss occurs at a very young age, like Emily. One of those things is that there was so little time for a child to make a significant mark on this earth. I can honestly say that that is not the case with Emily.

On the day before her last surgery, Emily had to have a tube placed down her nose and into her stomach for surgery preparation. She had had this procedure done to her so many times before, and it was always very frightening to her. Just before two nurses had to begin this procedure, Emily turned to me and said, "Mommy, why can't I just be an ordinary kid?" I said to her with complete sincerity that she could never be an ordinary kid because she was already extraordinary.

In reflecting on what I could say today about this extraordinary child, I thought of four lasting marks she left on not only my life but on many of you who are here today and knew her well. The first mark was to show me how to live life to the fullest. She loved life. I used to fear that the reason she had so much life in her was because she was not meant to be on this earth for long. I was right.

As a first-grader, she frequently had to copy sentences. Because she missed so much school, I would often make up sentences and she would copy them, but occasionally she would want to write her own sentences. One of those sentences always said, "I am happy." For those of you who looked through her first-grade journal yesterday at the funeral home, almost every page had the sentence, "I am happy." I often said to Bob, "How could she be happy with everything she has to endure?" She taught me that the answer was simple. She looked at her illness as an inconvenience and lived her life around it.

She did not allow this disease that would eventually take her life to ruin her time on earth. The result was that, however brief, she had a very happy and full life and brought so much joy to our lives. I think she had a very old soul because she understood what was really important in life at a very young age.

There is no answer to why this happened to our family and more particularly to our little girl. Yet she showed us that our lives could be changed in a minute, and because of that we needed to enjoy every moment of our time together on earth. If we had spent the last three and a half years being bitter, we would not have experienced some of our most cherished memories of Emily. The second mark was to show me how important it is to love yourself. Emily thought very highly of herself. In January, she came home from school after her class had discussed the importance of writing to our elected officials, and said, "Mommy, I have to write to President Clinton." The next day, Emily wrote that letter at Sloan-Kettering, while waiting to have a bone scan. In the letter, she told the president her name, and that she was a first-grader, and that she had a big brother named Matthew, and that she had a doll named Samantha and listed all of her closest friends. When I saw the tone of this letter, I said "Em, don't you want to ask the president some questions, maybe about the poor or children or education?" And she said, "No, I think I'll just tell him about myself." She signed the letter, "Your new friend, Emily Rice" and was angry when she didn't get an immediate response.

Because of chemotherapy, Emily lost her hair four times. Bob and I would worry about it affecting her self-esteem. We worried needlessly. Each time she lost her hair, we would reassure her that she was still the most beautiful little girl in the world, whether she had hair or not. She would always reply, "I know." While I think the last two times she was more self-conscious of the hair loss, she never let it mar her opinion of herself.

When she returned to preschool the first time after she lost her hair, she walked into the classroom, took off her hat and said to her classmates, "You see, I lost all my hair. It fell out because I had to take important medicine, but as soon as I finish it, it will grow back. So I don't want any of you to worry about me." At the age of four, she had managed to rest the minds of her peers and, more importantly, had removed the taboo of her hair loss all in one sentence. It was business as usual after that.

Just four weeks ago today, our family sat as part of the

congregation and watched our wonderful son receive his First Holy Communion. Emily had gotten a new outfit for the occasion, and she was quite taken with herself. She said to me, "You know, Mommy, I think I may be the prettiest girl there." I looked at my bald child who was so thin from so many surgeries and chemotherapy and said, "You know, honey, I am sure you will be."

I don't know how she could have endured what she went through without the high self-esteem she had for herself and the inner strength that came with it. She fought to survive to the day she died because in her heart she felt she was worth it. And she was.

Her third mark was to show me that when adversity strikes, continue to move forward. She never saw herself as sick, only as getting better. In March, after her eighth operation, Emily was in the hospital for nearly four weeks. During that time, she tried to keep up with her classwork because she wanted to return to school as soon as possible. One of her oncologists came in to talk, and she said to him, "I can't talk now. I'm taking a math test."

On May 14, while Bob and I were told that she would not survive, she was doing her homework. One of her assignments was to read a few sentences about two children who were sick with colds and answer questions that followed. One of the questions was "Are you sick now?" While receiving a blood transfusion and while unbeknownst to her, her parents were receiving the most unthinkable news about her fate, she responded to the question, "No, I am not sick now."

When Bob and I told her the next day that she would need another operation, she was so upset because she did not want to miss the performances of her class play about dinosaurs. They were held this week. Even during the last days of her life, she planned to return to school.

During the last ten days of her life, she wrote a letter to each of her classmates. On the Monday of Memorial Day weekend, while being attached to a morphine pump because of the pain she was in, she asked one of her doctors if she would be able to return to school on Wednesday.

Even while enduring nine operations, several protocols of chemotherapy, biological therapy and radiation, she never stopped planning and looking forward to her future. While I must give some credit to modern medical techniques, her will and her belief that she would someday be well and thus needed to plan ahead is what kept her alive for such a long time.

The last mark she made was to show me the importance of taking charge of your life. Emily called the shots until the end of her life. On the night of her last surgery, we were told that there was a possibility she would not live through the night. Immediately after coming to intensive care, Emily received the Sacraments of the Anointing of the Sick and Confirmation. Both Bob and I said that we were ready then for her to die. Within an hour and while on a ventilator, she mouthed to Bob "Movie." Bob deciphered that she wanted to watch *Space Jam* and began to go and put the movie in the VCR. She then began moving her right arm frantically, indicating that she wanted to write something. One of us gave her a pen and paper, and in a drugged stupor, she wrote "REW." She had enough presence of mind to let Bob know that she remembered that she had watched half the movie that morning and wanted him to rewind it to the beginning. She then proceeded to write down any thought that came to her mind. We are lucky she was only on the ventilator for eighteen hours because we had run out of paper. That pad is testament of how she was still in charge of her life, and she was not ready to go.

Emily spent six days in intensive care and returned to Memorial Hospital. During those first few days there, she was told countless times by family and staff how "great" and "wonderful" and "excellent" she was doing. Frankly, she was sick of hearing it because she told me that she didn't feel like any of those things. As she lay dying, she made up this list of things that you couldn't do in her room. The list included such things as:

"Don't say good."

"Don't say wonderful."

"Don't say great."

It also included such things as "No dancing," "No singing," "No kissing too much," and "No touching too much." It ended with the diplomatic sentence of "Now don't do this or else you're in trouble." She then asked me to tape it to her door. I must tell you that those rules were followed. A few nights before she died, she said to me "Mama, I'm so scared." I began kissing and hugging her and telling her not to be afraid. She then said to me, "Mom, the rule!"

More importantly, two of her doctors told me that the list made them realize how often they used those same words on their young patients. They had never thought that children may not want to hear such words of praise, particularly when they are not feeling well. They both said that because of the list they would be more conscious of what they said to those children they cared for.

In those last days, she had so little control of her life. She couldn't go to school, she couldn't see her friends, she couldn't even get out of bed. But she realized that she still

controlled that small hospital space, and she ruled it with an iron hand. For so long, when it began to appear that Emily would not survive this terrible disease, we prayed for a miracle. We prayed that, either through medical and/or divine intervention, those terrible cells would stop growing in her little body. It was only after we knew that she would not survive that I realized that we had the miracle all along — because she was the miracle.

While it was not what we were praying for, I realized that in her short life she had made an impact on so many lives by just being herself. To touch so many people in seven years was a miracle in itself. When you remember Emily, I ask you to remember these marks she made on mine and so many other lives. I ask you to assimilate them into your everyday life, in her memory. There is no better way to remember her. Emily taught us about how to live life by teaching through the best method known: her example.

Part III

Lessons

A New Perspective

Ellen Goodman, columnist with the *Boston Globe*, wrote an article shortly after one of our country's school shootings, entitled "Hurrying Healing" (see Part IV, Section A). In it she asked why we as a society or culture are fixated on immediate healing. Why aren't we spending any time grieving, mourning, talking about the pain, feeling it, memorializing it, remembering it? She wondered why every clergyperson and psychologist interviewed by the media talked about getting to healing before the dead were buried, while the parents and friends of these children were in the grip of pain, shock and devastation. She thought these grieving individuals needed to talk about their loss, to ask "why," to scream or pound something, or to hold each other and sob. She also thought they would need to do that over and over during the coming months and years—that is, if anyone will let them.

Goodman also asked if healing is possible without mourning, the work of grief and the painful process of putting lives

back together with the gaping hole left by their losses. The
track record of lives filled with repressed grief testifies that
healing does not come without grieving. Watch people at
funerals who barely knew the deceased struggle to keep
back the tears, contain the emotion. Mention a child's name
to parents five or ten years after the child's death and watch
the invisible walls of steel fall over their faces or the never-
ending veil of tears begin again. Talk to teenagers who have
lived through their own suicide attempt and listen to the
losses that robbed them of enough hope to go on living.

We, as adults, have passed on this message of instant
healing in our culture. Children, thankfully, are still open to
questioning, searching, feeling and dealing with the emotions and thoughts surrounding death, trauma, divorce and
other life-changing losses. Perhaps in earlier times, it was
even the children who helped the adults process the pain
and dilemma of it all. Before our relocation and mobility
patterns made wanderers of us all and separated families,
there was always someone in the family to whom a kid could
talk. When extended families lived on the farm or in the
same neighborhood, you could walk to Grandma's or Uncle
Mike's and ask about death in the same way a kid could ask
how cows make milk, or why leaves die. People expected
kids to ask questions, and in the answering both the child
and the adult were addressing the issue together, processing
it, feeling it together. But today our time is too scheduled
and neither Grandma nor Uncle Mike lives within walking
distance. Thus, kids are left by default in the precarious care
of their peer group. Who do they model? The adults who
are hurrying to healing or their friends who are willing to
walk down this painful path with them. Where is the adult
understanding, wisdom, life experience that can attest to

living through the hard times? To complicate this issue of establishing who does this work, we have become a specialized society. Teachers think parents should handle grief and parents think the clergy should and no one wants to invade anyone's privacy when "it's not my place" to do so. Because of this trend, we have children copying children when there is a suicide. Perhaps it is because the children are the only ones available to talk to after death or tragedy strikes.

Sadly now, we as a country have experienced a barrage of violent deaths in our schools. The tragedy of children killing children and teachers presents an entirely different type of grief. This is not one of just sadness and longing; it is fused with anger, outrage, guilt and blame. Here the old adages do not apply. We need more than modeling; we need education on handling these powerful experiences of loss and grief. All of us. The fact is we lose too many of our school-age children each year. In addition, teachers and parents die, too. Families are decimated. Friends are depressed. Schools battered.

When a teenager was killed by a train the day after high school graduation, the principal responded to a newspaper reporter's question, "What are you going to do?" by saying, "School is out, the kids are gone, there's nothing we can do." I ended up working with this school and know that the principal and everyone there *wanted* to do something, but like most of their colleagues in schools across the country, they didn't know what to do. So much of a student's life gets played out at school, and more time is spent in relationships with peers and people in school than in actual family time. Yet no one at school knows substantially more than parents about handling grief and loss, and the toll this takes on our children. Most universities with programs in school

counseling, psychology and social work address this topic in
one course or a part of a course. Most departments of education offer instruction on death and dying in the psychology or child development or family life courses. These
usually fall into an elective course category, and, even when
addressing the grieving process, they seldom address the
issue of grief over time. People who work in schools see the
effects of grief played out over time and watch helplessly
the decline in student learning and involvement. They often
are able to pinpoint the time when a student begins to
decline or to withdraw or to "medicate" himself or herself
against their pain, and this is always long after the "event"
has passed.

The work of helping students grieve in schools is ongoing. It calls on the school to expand its role as a school
family, providing a safe place for this work to take place. In
this space, students can learn to understand what is happening to them instead of only acting out feelings or
repressing them, becoming depressed or hurting themselves. A grief and loss team can provide interventions and
ongoing strategies that can help restore health and healing
after the counselors from the surrounding schools have
gone. Those who desire to do this work also know that we
need a team of players. Caring, concerned teachers have
tried to help wherever they can, and they know better than
any of us that it is too hard to do alone. They also know this
work calls for a new philosophy. It requires poking a hole in
a long-held taboo of not discussing grief. If we can discuss
alcohol and drug addictions and sexually transmitted diseases, then we ought to be able to discuss grief. The following suggestions for training provide a direction and
format for those who want to do grief work with students,

including teachers, administrators, students, parents and
community members, because all of us want to do something, and everyone can.

All new proposals for schools meet the brick wall of "we
don't have the money or the time to do it." This proposal for
intervention does not take money, but it does take time. The
time element cannot be quantified. Sometimes it's a lot,
sometimes very little. This book proposes a strategy for
helping students understand what loss and trauma, tragedy
and death do to us and finding ways to do more than cope.
The rest of this book contains everything needed to begin
this work and train the team. The people who will find the
time are the people who have a heart for the work and likely
have encountered profound grief in their own lives. They
are the ones who have watched our young people suffer
alone, or medicate their pain or question the value of their
own lives following a loss or trauma in the school community. They have waited a long time to do something, and
they usually jump at the opportunity to do it, all the while
repeating an insecure mantra like "I really don't have any
training or experience and I don't know what to do." But if
the heart and the will are there, the time will be available,
too. While the author is available for consulting and speaking and training, her presence and her fee are not necessary.
The worksheets and all updated information in the future
will be available on our Web site *www.kidsgrieve.org*. So, the
price of the book, time with the office copier, the cost of
paper and, perhaps, coffee for the teams are the only expen-
ditures needed to begin. The biggest expenses, of course,
will come out of the account known as the "Hearts and
Souls of the Workers," and that group probably will buy the
book out of their own pockets.

TEAM MEMBERS AND TRAINING

The best way to determine the team membership is to give a workshop that is not mandatory but open to all staff. The people who show up and express an interest will become the pool from which the team will be formed. The agenda for this workshop (see Part IV, Section B) can include an overview of the philosophical approach and training recommended in the book, as well as the "characteristics of healthy grieving" list. For those interested, a commitment to training is a requirement for membership on the team. While a variety of people may be interested in serving, the majority of team members need to be on staff mainly because they are "there" every day. Since we cannot predict when the need for grief interventions will arise, some member of the team needs to be available. So teachers likely will make up the majority of the team memberships, along with school nurses, counselors and administrative staff. While there certainly is room for parents, perhaps students, and other community professionals in certain circumstances, time and proximity will present a challenge to them participating fully.

If the superintendent in Waldwick, New Jersey, asked me to put together a team for Carolyn's school I could guess with a pretty high degree of accuracy which staff members would participate. If we invited any outside personnel it would likely be Father Bill Dowd of St. Luke's Church, Marian Brovero and Cyndie Rice. They are exceptional individuals with both the heart and desire to participate, and they would make the time. Father Bill works with kids from elementary school to senior high and beyond. St. Luke's runs one of the most successful intramural athletic programs in the area for boys and girls of all ages. Father

Bill already is a member of the Crisis Management team in town and has enthusiastically worked with members of the parish to start grief support groups and workshops. If students knew he was available every Tuesday after school in the guidance office, I'd bet next week's church collection they would show up in droves. Marian is a recently retired teacher who is revered by the community. Her son Ray died when he was just a young man. She could have become bitter. Instead she became an even better teacher, with an unrivaled heart and compassion for kids. Cyndie Rice is a young, energetic, cool mom, who also is a lawyer and has been a school board member. She is involved in the community and is trusted by kids and their parents. She and her husband also lost their beautiful daughter Emily to a rare form of cancer when she was in the first grade. Her eulogy is in Part II. Cyndie shared her grief with this community and has been a model for remembering and honoring the lives of those we love who are gone from our presence. Her participation on a team would be an extension of the way that she and her husband, and their son Matt and daughter Hope, have honored Emily's life. These three community members are trusted, respected and liked by kids. So they would be an appropriate exception to having mostly staff members on the team. I am certain there are such exceptional people in every school community across the country who would be similarly great assets.

A NOTE ABOUT PARENTS

In a sadly repetitive spring ritual of warm nights and inexperienced drivers, combined with prom parties and graduation celebrations, people die, mostly our children. Parents are all too aware of this fact. They lay awake during those nights with memories of spring nights past, hoping, praying that their children will be safe. They hover only at the edge of sleep until they hear the garage door open or the lock turn. Whether there actually is a death or a gnawing fear of one, parents seem to bear the burden of worry over the safety of all of our kids, especially their own. It creates a gnawing feeling that we hope is not a premonition. This empty feeling of sadness and longing, however, can easily be pushed down as everyone gives way to busy schedules, celebrations, and keeping one step ahead in the parenting game.

When there is a death, parents grab their children and are secretly thankful that it was not theirs who died. Many report that the next feeling is guilt for feeling thankful that it was someone else's child and not their own. Next, they typically want to spare their children the pain of grief but that, of course, is impossible. No one is spared. The question is only if the parents will go through it together with their children. Parents are the linchpin in this work. They can support it or undo it. Endorse it or demean it. Participate in it or demand it. And their support, endorsement and participation are vital to the success of the endeavor. It can take place without them, but the power of their support is immeasurable. When students are interviewed after being involved in drug abuse they repeatedly say that what made the most difference in their struggle to survive was "what their parents said." Now, for those of us who are parents, this comes as a shock. The feeling that we might as well be talking to a brick wall when we try to advise our children, especially our teenagers, is well-documented by parents around the world and down through the ages. But even their tacit approval is helpful, even if they do not want to be involved at all. Remember that we are they, and it is hard for us to help our children grieve if we have not dealt with our own grief. And every-one agrees that we all have more unresolved grief than resolved. So it's going to be a struggle for parents, too.

TEAM-TRAINING GUIDELINES

Characteristics of Healthy Grieving

These characteristics form the basis for team-training sessions, topics for training, and our philosophy and orientation for helping us as well as others who are grieving.

REALIZING . . .
that everyone experiences loss

RECOGNIZING . . .
that grief is a natural human response to loss

REMEMBERING . . .
our losses and how they affect our lives in healthy and unhealthy ways

REDEFINING . . .
the way we view loss and its consequences in ourselves and in others

REDEEMING . . .
loss through positive acts of love and service instead of self-defeating reactions

First Team-Training Session:
REALIZING that everyone experiences loss

Dear Team,

We cannot help others with the losses they experience, until we are willing to acknowledge, remember and process our own. Loss can come in many forms: death, divorce, traumatic events, debilitating conditions and other tragedies. They become central events in our lives because of the changes and gaps and holes they leave in their wake. Grief is a powerful, sometimes overwhelming, collection of responses that we experience as a result of loss. It effects nearly every dimension of our lives: emotional, psychological, physical, mental and spiritual. It effects the way we think and feel and trust. It changes what we have believed in, counted on and thought was constant. We all have experienced loss. We all grieve, some of us more than others, few of us well. Our hearts ache for those we know who are grieving, because we know how it feels and we want to make it all better.

I am not suggesting that our losses become the focus of our work, but they certainly are the starting place for us both individually and as a team. The reason this is the cornerstone of grief work is that we need to be able to separate our grief from that of another, and we cannot do that without starting with our own. You would not be here if you did not have a heart for the grieving, and the best way we can help others is to learn to navigate that fine line between their pain and ours. This vital ingredient in any meaningful contact or counsel is called empathy, which means being in touch with the pain in your own life to the extent that it evokes compassion and understanding for another's life. It is different from sympathy, which is kind and helpful, but does not have the far-reaching effects of the empathic response.

An effective way to talk about the losses in our lives is to generate a list of all the losses we can think of that have affected us, or others we know. Every loss mentioned is important. No loss is insignificant.

ACTIVITY: GENERATE LIST OF PERSONAL AND/OR FAMILY LOSSES

You need a leader for this activity who can call on people and keep order. Assign someone to write on the board. It is best if this person's writing is legible. The leader and recorder can be the same person if your group is small. Then brainstorm as a group to construct a list that will include losses you have experienced personally or those of which you have heard. Remember the rules of brainstorming:

- One person speaks at a time.
- No one can comment on any contribution.
- When there are no further contributions, discussion can take place.

Everyone else needs to write the list on the worksheet (Part IV, Section B) as you will use this in subsequent group meetings. Start with "death" and "divorce," and you are off and running. When the group list is complete, ask what people thought of and wouldn't say, or what people have written down that was important for them but thought it wouldn't be for the group. For example, a common experience that is often not shared is the loss of a pet.

Next, I suggest that you look at your own list and place a checkmark by the ones you have experienced personally or with your closest friends or family members. Then I want members of the group to think about an important loss in their own lives that can be shared with the group in one to three sentences. If the team is larger than three, do this first in dyads or triads, then with the whole group.

Now, I want to speak to each one of you personally, and the best way I can do that in absentia is for someone in the group to read what follows aloud.

First, I want you to know how proud I am to be working on the same "team" with you. You are brave. Even though you may not be feeling so after sharing your losses, trust me you are indeed. The loss and grief we have experienced can bring us to our knees and leave us feeling anything but brave. Still, I say you are brave because, in spite of how difficult this is for all of us, you are here. Remember that no two losses are the same, similar perhaps, but not the same. Even when you share the same loss in common with others, it is still different for each of us, because the relationships were different. Yet, as human creatures we are alike in many ways. We all have tear ducts. We all experience anger, rejection, sadness and longing, along with laughter, peace and satisfaction. But there is an "aloneness" in grief that is inescapable. That is why no one can mean it when they say, "I know how you feel," because no one does. Next, I want to tell you that if you are wondering if you are "out of your league" or had a bout with temporary insanity when you volunteered for this work, you are wrong. Remember, if you have the heart, compassion and empathy, you have the needed experience to be here. We will answer the "What do I do" and "What do I say" questions as we go along.

Second Team-Training Session:

RECOGNIZING that grief is a natural human response to loss

Whenever we suffer a loss, there are always powerful emotions, responses and ripple effects that are natural human reactions. Let's talk about a few. When my husband died at age twenty-four, I also lost my friend, lover, high school sweetheart, partner, sole provider, confidant and father of my children. I was a mess. I was not able to function, even reasonably well, for months. So my children not only lost their father, but they also lost their mother, as they had known her. I was no longer the happy, enthusiastic, fun-loving mom they had experienced. I lost my self-confidence. I was scared, fearful of how we would live and whether or not I could do a good job raising my children alone. Children can sense all this, even if they don't understand exactly what is happening or why things are as they are.

We also were moving into our first house in September and Bob died on August 23. I had no means of supporting us financially, and I certainly could not pay a mortgage without him. So, I lost my first home before we even moved in. I felt cheated, robbed. I had spent the entire summer reupholstering old furniture and making drapes and curtains for every room in the house. I gave it all away, except one little ruffled valance from my daughter's room. It seemed to be the only tangible piece of the life we would have had in that house. I told my friends to give everything to the new owners, and if they did not want them to burn them. Having a nice house became an aching obsession for me, and it took many long years to work that out.

Some of the components of loss are not immediately obvious to others, but they leave big holes in our lives. There are often things that we think no one else would understand or that we don't have the right to feel. Some don't even reach a conscious level in our thinking, and all we feel is a tremendous sense of longing. That longing can pervade our happiness and sense of well-being. I remember making a cup of hot chocolate for my brother-in-law one day and watched the satisfaction of longing come over his face. His mother, who had been dead for years, had taught me how to make hot chocolate. By following her recipe, I gave him back a little part of something he missed from the winter breakfasts fixed by his mom over the years. So, whether big or small, current or long past, the multiple accompanying changes that come with loss make up a large part of our grief. Everyone has stories like this, and most of us keep them to ourselves. So by asking about these accompanying losses, we can help students acknowledge their longing and walk with them through it.

The most important part of this training session is acknowledging that it is normal to experience disappointment and fear, longing and regret, heartache and anger, and a wide variety of emotions. It is a natural human response to miss what we have lost and can never regain. This acknowledgment is key to learning to live with loss and working through our grief.

A helpful way to talk about the effects of our life's losses is to embellish our list of losses with accompanying feelings or the ripple effects we experience as a result of the losses. Every effect mentioned is important. No effect is insignificant.

ACTIVITY: GENERATE LIST OF EFFECTS FROM OUR LOSSES

Here again you will need a leader for this activity who can encourage and organize participants' input. Take the list of losses that we generated in the first training session and brainstorm accompanying losses or ripple effects. It is often these very things that will be reported by a grieving person when asked, "What is the hardest part today?" So, when working with students, we have to become astute listeners, even to the small details, because it is easier to talk about something small and seemingly innocuous, as in Wes's story with his family dog, than to deal with the larger reality. It is important to listen to every story knowing they are telling us something about themselves and their pain or fears.

A helpful way to handle this activity visually is by "webbing," which is a tool we use when teaching students to write and to expand their ideas. Write a loss on the board; draw a circle around it with little lines coming out from the circle like a spider's web. Write the resulting or accompanying losses on the lines coming out from the main or central loss. For example, think about Wes and his dog. He and his family had lost the ability to discuss his illness with each other. The looming loss before them was his life. One of their accompanying losses was their inability to communicate freely with him, to "be" with him as they had always been. Remember the little boy at Carolyn's school whose grandfather died six weeks after Carolyn's death? One of the things he loved most about his grandfather was how athletic, active and involved he was in the Winter Games in Lake Placid. In addition to being a starter and timer at the Winter Olympics, he had given his grandchildren entrance to the events and lift passes to ski. One of the accompanying losses in this boy's life was the exciting adventures this man gave to his grandchildren.

After this exercise, write or share aloud (with someone taking notes) the ripple effects of loss that you had never thought of before. The worksheet for this is in Part IV, Section B. Keep this insight in your hip pocket, because this will be one of the keys you will use to unlock conversations with your students.

ADDITIONAL ACTIVITY

Choose a couple of stories in this book and research them for accompanying losses and emotional responses. If the information is not spelled out, decide what they could be.

Third Team-Training Session:

REMEMBERING our losses and how they affect our lives in healthy and unhealthy ways

Remembering is the heart of grief work. If we don't remember our losses and the ways they have changed our lives, we are destined to live with unresolved grief. Unresolved grief is unhealthy and requires tremendous energy to control. It changes our lives in ways that require years and too much energy to undo. Living out an existence characterized by bitterness or fear, hardened hearts or resentment, depression and withdrawal is a life no one intentionally sets out to live. But we resist processing our grief, because it requires remembering and that brings up uncomfortable emotions and that lets loose our grief. And we are not comfortable as a culture or as people with those powerful responses. We fear it all getting loose. We aren't sure we can control it if loosed. So we practice showing no emotion, saying we are fine and pretending to be so. That is the work of forgetting, which is going in an opposite and unhealthy direction from remembering. But the old adage warns us that if we forget we are doomed to repeat, and that applies here also. So if we have managed to suppress one loss, we think erroneously that we can keep doing so. Unresolved grief, however, will and must find its resolve, and unless we carefully tend to the changes that loss brings to our lives, they will change us.

Fortunately, children are good at remembering. I watched

a little girl remember on Christmas Eve this year and, with classic innocence, she helped her mother remember. Because I had been at Carolyn's school for three months, I wound up doing the last of my shopping on Christmas Eve and one stop was at the Barnes and Noble bookstore, where I had a book signing the week before Carolyn died. The woman who arranged the signing saw me, and we exchanged holiday greetings. Then she said, "Hey, while you are here, why don't you sign the books we have on the shelves?" I agreed and stood at the information desk signing this stack of books. A woman came to the desk for information, and I was the only one there. We smiled at each other, and I kept signing. Pretty soon she said, "I gather that is your book."

I laughed and said, "Yes, I swear it is."

She laughed, too, and asked, "What's it about?"

When I told her it was a book about helping people grieve, she said, "That sounds interesting." Then she paused, as though trying to think of a way to relate, before saying, "No one in our family is grieving."

I said, "Well, that's good. Merry Christmas."

She said the same back to me, and a clerk came to answer her inquiry. When she was finished with her business, she turned to me and said, "Good luck with your book."

I said, "Thank you," but she didn't leave.

She kind of shook her head and said, "You know, I don't know anybody who's grieving."

I said, "Boy! That's terrific. But if the need arises, my book is called *Mourning and Dancing*, and it is a book you could give to anyone who has suffered a loss."

Now, all of this time her daughter was standing next to

her mother, with her chin on her hand. She let her arm drop and said, "What about Mrs. Schmidt?"

This startled her mother, who turned and looked at her daughter like she was surprised to find her standing there and said, "Oh my word! Mary!"

I said, "Who is Mary?"

The daughter replied, "Our next-door neighbor."

The mother picked up on the memory and said, "Her husband died in early November. He was my husband's boss. They are wonderful neighbors and have been like second parents to us. She is really in tough shape, especially with the holidays here and all."

"I'm so sorry," I said, now feeling a little awkward that she might feel pressured to buy one of my books for Mary. So, I said, "Well, remember the name *Mourning and Dancing*, and you may want to get this for her later."

"Couldn't she use it now?" she asked.

Still feeling a little awkward about promoting a book sale, I said, "Sure . . . but either way."

Now, to make a long story a little shorter, she did buy a book, and I signed it for Mary and wrote it in memory of her husband. When I handed this woman my book, I noticed the tears in her eyes. I asked her if she was okay, and she said, now with full emotion in her voice, "This will be only my second Christmas without my father."

I put my arms around her, and she cried for a few minutes in the middle of the Barnes and Noble bookstore on Christmas Eve. I told her that I was so glad I had been there today and got to meet her and her daughter, who I had now included in our hug. I told them to share extra time and love with Mary and to do it in memory of their father and grandfather. And in the remembering of him they would feel his presence in their holidays, rather than a void that no one addresses.

Then I said, "Remembering helps us feel like we are put back together in some places. Candles can help you do this, too. If you buy a fat candle, or two if you want to give one to Mary, you can light it every morning and blow it out at the end of the day during the holidays." I went on to suggest the candles in a jar, and we talked about the warmth of candlelight and the symbolism of the flame for love or eternal light. I told them that if they do this intentionally, thinking of and remembering their loved ones, they will include those who cannot be present in their holiday rituals. I also reminded them to put a note on the back door that says "blow out the candle," so they wouldn't burn the house down when they go out.

They smiled at each other, and I suggested that they read the book before they give it to Mary. They agreed to that idea and thanked me again. Then they walked off, arm in arm.

As I drove home, I thought about the sense of longing so many people tell me characterizes their holidays. And I wondered why we resist remembering, when it can restore us and reconnect us to that which is gone and ease some of that longing. I went home and got out all of the angel ornaments people at the school gave me in Carolyn's memory and put them on the tree. This encounter at the bookstore reminded me of how we need to be intentional about remembering.

When my niece Jodi was a junior in high school, she survived a car accident in which her dear friend Cheryl was killed. Five years later on her wedding day, Jodi and Brad arranged to have a limousine come to the house an hour before the wedding. Then, dressed in their wedding finery, they took an extra bridesmaid bouquet to the cemetery and put it on Cheryl's grave. This gift of remembering Cheryl included her in the wedding celebration and their new life together, instead of trying to find ways not to think about her absence. Consider how great a gift this was to Cheryl's family, who were present at the wedding and would have given anything to see their daughter walk down that aisle.

In Mandy's story, the barn became a place of remembrance. It helped her family and friends remember to remember her. The barn became a place where kids could do something to process their grief and honor Mandy's life. Her friend Jason wrote about the experience of losing Mandy and in his writing remembered everything about her that was dear to him. Carolyn's tree in the All-Purpose Room at her school became a vehicle for children to remember her and all she gave them. The students at Columbine High School put flowers and notes on a chain-link fence and on cars in acts of remembering and honoring their friends. I thought it would have been helpful to locate a space around the school property to build memorial sites for each student who died there and connect them with a stone or brick walkway. There students could go even years later to remember. Mandy's own remembrance of her friend Amity put her in touch with peace in her soul. Remembering gave her confidence and comfort about going to a better place. Knowing she felt and believed in that confidence brings comfort today to those who knew her. Mandy's written tribute to her friend Amity is in Part IV, Section E.

Remembering, even the horrible or traumatic losses in our lives, can help put us back together again in some respects. The word "re-member" actually means just that, with "re" meaning "again" or "repeat," as in redo, rework, replay, and "member" being a part of the whole, be it our whole self, or family, or class or team. So, remembering in grief work is an intentional activity to honor the loss we have experienced and the way in which it has affected our life. Even when a loss has robbed us of trust or innocence or confidence, we can honor the part of the experience that produced growth in our lives, like wisdom, compassion and understanding. This then becomes the source of empathy for helping others, which we will talk about in a later training session on redeeming our losses.

ACTIVITY: HELP STUDENTS REMEMBER TO REMEMBER

Under the encouragement of the group leader, the team can share ideas that will heighten their awareness for responding to remembrance opportunities and designing creative activities. By reminding each other about common, opportune moments that occur in the school day and by sharing ideas about responses, the team can become equipped for the task of creating reminders for students to remember their losses. In future encounters students will find many chances to do the important emotional work of grieving that comes when they remember. Talking about a loss or death or divorce or injury is the obvious way to remember, but there are others. Brainstorm as a group and see how many ways you can suggest. Then discuss as a group ways you can intentionally determine times and activities to do this important processing.

After Joby Greene was killed, his friend and classmate, Cory, wrote about his death two years later. When I spoke to Cory and asked why he wrote this story, he said it was because he did not want to forget what happened. He also wanted everyone to remember what good friends Sean and Joby were, especially since Sean was driving the other vehicle in the accident. Joby's mother, who is a teacher, has created two places where students can remember. One is a wall of honor in Joby's high school, where pictures and scholarship awards and plaques of honor are placed in memory of all of the students who had died. Then she created a garden, much like the one we have at Carolyn's school, that has become a working memorial for her and anyone who wants to come and dig around in precious memories and bring new things to life. All of the members of Joby's graduating class wore green ribbons to honor their friend Joby Greene and left a chair empty to remember his place in their class. Then, in the years that followed, Joby's friends named a "hang-out" room in the attic of a friend's garage the "Greene Room," so they can remember that Joby has a place in their group and in their hearts.

Tom Searches for His Father's Plaque

Note: *When schools decide to create a memorial, to facilitate this remembering process, one of the primary considerations should be permanence. A memorial tree that dies is worse than no tree at all. Instead of symbolizing life and everlasting memories, the dead tree is like salt in a wound, causing unnecessary pain instead of comfort. Plaques that tarnish and become illegible become an insult, not a fitting memorial. The following is a story written by my son, Tom, after he went searching for the memorial a high school chose for his father.*

The whole idea of "fatherhood" has been a curiosity for as much of my life as I can remember. I was born to Bob and Sally Downham, the second of two children. My sister Tamara is three years older than I. My story really begins even before I can remember.

My folks were high school sweethearts and were married during my dad's freshman year in college. At Butler University, he was a multisport athlete and played both offense and defense for legendary coach Tony Hinkle. My dad had always said he knew exactly what he wanted to do with his life. He wanted to have a family, and he wanted to be a coach. By August 1967, he accomplished that goal. He was named the head football coach for Elwood High School and was a husband and father. I was not yet two years old.

Now, fast forward thirty years. I am married and live in Fort Wayne, Indiana. My wife Lisa and I have a son, Aaron Robert. Recently, I was visiting a client of mine in Tipton, Indiana. As I traveled west on Rt. 28 heading toward I-69 to go back to Fort Wayne, I drove past a sign welcoming visitors to Elwood. I had some time, and, having never been there since we left as a kid, I decided to stop. More specifically, I wanted to find the high school, in search of my dad's press box, which he built the summer he died. The story goes that after his death, they had a ceremony at halftime of a football game and put a plaque on the structure dedicating it to my father. This was something I wanted to see. When I found the school the first thing I saw was an enormous, newly built football stadium. I found some guys out working near one of the maintenance buildings and introduced myself. Although they were older they knew nothing of the story of my dad or of his press box. They said that the athletic director might be up at the school and he may have

further information. I drove up to the school, which was
also very new and modern and found the AD's office,
appropriately next to the gym. I walked in and introduced
myself.

"Hi. My name is Tom Downham. I didn't mean to inter-
rupt, but many years ago my dad was the football coach
here."

The AD said, "He sure was! I knew your dad. As a matter of fact, I was the manager for his team my senior year."

Now, I don't want to give the impression that he was all
excited to see me at first. But, I am not much older than my
dad was when he died, and since I look a lot like him, the
combination kind of spooks people. To this day, I am
amazed by the reaction that people have when they are
taken back to August 1967. Only now am I beginning to
understand what a loss it must have been for them.

I asked Mike about the press box and the plaque. He said
he thought that the structure built by my dad had been
moved and was now the press box by the baseball stadium.
He knew about the plaque but was not sure if it survived
the move. As we hopped in my car to drive around to the
baseball stadium, Mike told me that the new football stadium was built in the late 1970s. I saw how enormous it was
as we drove past it. It is a large white structure that can seat
a few thousand visitors, with locker rooms, concession
stands and a very long press box on top of it. The letters
spelling out "Home of the Panthers" must have been twelve
to fifteen feet tall. The north end of the football stadium
faced the baseball field. Mike explained that the top section
of my father's structure had been moved by crane about six
hundred yards and placed on a new cinderblock foundation.
He kept saying that he thought that the plaque was still

there, but he wasn't sure. We got out of my car and walked
to the structure behind home plate. I noticed that the base
of the press box had relatively new aluminum siding. I was
prepared to find that the plaque was covered up or no
longer there because . . . well, it has been a while.

"Yep, there it is," Mike said.

I walked up the stairs and stood looking at the two-foot-
square sign. It looked like so many others I had seen, sort of
historical landmarks. I thought to myself how many people
must have looked at it and pondered, "I wonder who that
guy was?" I noticed that the siding had been cut very nicely
around the sign. Someone who also didn't know who that
guy was, but thought, "If it's here, it must mean something
to someone" probably did it. Somehow that touched me.
The sign was very simple:

In Memory of   **Robert H. Downham**   **Teacher and Coach**   **1967**

Wow, that was thirty years ago! For the first time in my
life I stood in front of a historical sign that was actually my
history. Mike said that he remembered when my dad went
to the FCA camp. He said, "He was in pretty bad shape
when he came back."

I said, "Yeah, but I understand he was feeling pretty good
about where he was with his Maker."

Mike nodded.

I stood there and talked very comfortably with this
person I had known for all of ten minutes. At one point he

paused and looked around and said, "Well, this is something. . . ." For some reason, I really wanted to be there that night when he went home and told his wife that I stopped by. Here we were, at the sight of my "quest for the Holy Grail," and all I wanted to do was get to know this guy. Unfortunately, the school had an activity starting in fifteen minutes and he needed to be there. While walking back to the car I asked, "So, do I look like my dad?"

Mike did a spit take and said, "Shoot, yes!"

When we got back to the gym we exchanged business cards, and he told me all about the school. He said that he thought that Bob would have been proud of how far Elwood High School had come since he was here.

Then out of nowhere he said, "And by looking at you, I can tell he would be proud of you as well."

What a moment of confirmation. Two days later I received a yellow envelope in the mail from Mike. With it was an old eight-by-ten glossy of my dad and a note saying that Mike knew there were some old pictures around, and they actually had two of these. He wanted me to have one. He also told me that there are a couple of other players from my dad's last team who still are involved with the school. Now I can look forward to meeting them. I'll have to make sure that I make it back to Tipton again, so I can visit Elwood.

Fourth Team-Training Session:

REDEFINING the way we view loss and its consequences in ourselves and in others

In the previous sessions we identified the losses that we have experienced and encountered, the importance of empathy in our work and being able to separate ourselves from another's experience, while holding on to the losses of our own lives as touchstones. Then we explored the valuable work of remembering. Now we want to talk about how our culture has helped or hindered us in the process of learning to live with loss.

When Mike Landis was killed in a car accident on the way to a college bowl game, his sixteen-year-old daughter was driving. The roads in this part of Georgia are flat and straight and Mike was feeling sleepy. So he told Laura she could drive while he took a nap. As he settled into the passenger seat, he reminded her to awaken him if she got tired. She let him sleep. She was wide-awake, had good music on and the driving was easy. There was nothing she could have done to prevent the accident. A highly intoxicated driver crossed six lanes of traffic and hit them head-on, primarily on the passenger side of the car. Laura's physical injuries were not life-threatening. She was released the next day from the hospital.

Mike was a teacher and athletic director at the high school Laura attended. She and her dad were together daily. She was his only child. Her mother, Deb, attested to their close, wonderful relationship. So what does Laura do with those horrifying memories of her father's death? Everyone keeps telling her, if they dare to speak at all about the accident, that there was nothing she could have done and she should try not to think about it. Not think about it? Is that even possible? Laura says "no." Right now, the accident is the most overwhelmingly powerful memory she has when she thinks of her dad. If she tries to "forget" it, then she blots out all of her other memories of him, too, because no memory of her dad can come into her mind without the memory of the accident. So, I encouraged her to "remember" it, even though it is painful to do so. She needs to remember it, replay it, reconfigure it, until she comes to the conclusion herself that it was indeed an accident. That it happened in a split second and there was no time to do anything. But she has to come to that conclusion herself or she won't believe it. She won't be able to remember the good things or the happy times with her dad, until she has worked through and processed the accident, and that takes time.

My niece, Lindsay, is one of Laura's friends. She called me to ask what she could do to help, and I said that she should let Laura feel badly for a while. I encouraged Lindsay to express understanding: that it was a horrible thing and that it seems normal that anyone who went through such a tragedy would feel awful for a while. I suggested that she set up a time for them to talk regularly, perhaps while walking or exercising. I reminded this good friend that Laura would have a difficult time focusing on her studies and a study group could be a great help. Redefining the way we view our losses is critical to healing.

Members of the team should be prepared to help students

begin the process of redefining their losses in new ways, rather than applying unhealthy cliches.

ACTIVITY: HOW SOCIETY ENCOURAGES AND DISCOURAGES THE GRIEVING PROCESS

This activity can be completed either as an individual task or as a shared experience. Develop a list of the ways that our modern culture both encourages and discourages us to process our grief. Thinking about the steps we've taken thus far, in what ways does the culture realize that loss is universal, recognize that grief is natural, and allow us to remember the losses we've experienced? The list can be generated privately and then shared aloud with the group or can be developed by the group as a whole. The list can include clichés and admonitions that are common to our social mores and directives given to us by others, either directly or implied. When the list is complete, rate each item as either encouraging or discouraging. This may be the beginning of your list of things to say or not to say, do or not do.

Remember that as we came through the challenges of the twentieth century, we reinforced the "pull yourself up by your bootstraps" philosophy. We survived the world wars and the Great Depression with musical directives like "Put On a Happy Face," "Smile Though Your Heart Is Breaking" and "Keep Your Sunny Side Up." Then as we moved through the 1960s and 1970s and the Vietnam War, we began to understand post-traumatic stress and lives of quiet desperation. And the self-help movement was born. With this advent also came support groups. While

Alcoholics Anonymous was started in the 1930s it did not become a household word until other Twelve-Step programs were spawned using this effective model. The emphasis on getting healed and becoming healthy has spilled over into the areas of fitness, vitamins, food, habits and positive thinking. The area of grief and learning to live with loss has not moved ahead much, but there are pioneers in this field and some national organizations. Let's see how much we know.

ACTIVITY: EQUIP THE TEAM WITH GOOD RESOURCES

On the board write the following questions and ask what the group knows:

1. Who is Elisabeth Kubler-Ross?
2. What is Compassionate Friends?
3. Who is Earl Grollman?

Next, make a list of the books, videos or other resources that you have seen and *know* are helpful to people in grief. List any groups or resources you have available in your local community to which you can refer people or contact for helping the team. As a group, talk about what directives, models or expectations society still espouses and that impede the process of redefining the grief experience.

Note: More information, including a bibliography, is available in Part IV. New material and updated resources are always available on the Web at *www.kidsgrieve.org.* In fact, you are encouraged to share your own experiences with others on the Web site.

Several books are available that include curricula on how

to help children and teenagers cope with loss. It will be a part of the team's job to review all the resources and distinguish the best sources for information and materials. For example, the popular "Rainbows for All Children" by Marta and Laz includes lessons, program formats, volunteer training directives, lesson plans and workbooks. When a school purchases these materials, they also purchase the training package for school personnel, parents or interested community members. Most other books on grief are designed for helping children in a counseling/clinical/therapeutic setting, implying that professional counselors and therapists, who have some training in the field, will do the work. The work we are recommending, however, is done by the willing, most of whom have no training at all. All prepackaged lessons, activities and workbooks may be helpful in preparing the team, but the most important ingredient in all grief work is the person directing the process and the interactions. Aside from "Rainbows," there is little readily available for training trainers. It is for this group of people this book is written. The team should conduct its own reviews in order to recommend current grief books, programs and curriculum. This research will enhance the training of the people on the team who will work with students, individually or in group settings.

Some of this investigative work can be done either individually or in pairs between now and the next training session. Then everyone can report back to the group at large on their findings. So a follow-up meeting can include some information-sharing on redefining how we view the grief process. Once everyone has reported, there is one more culminating activity. Using a chalkboard or two sheets of chart paper, the group needs to make two lists: the unhealthy messages/strategies that have prevailed in our society and the healthy strategies inherent in this new philosophy and movement.

Redefining usually requires a change of attitude, and attitude is a funny little tune that we whistle in our minds and hearts. Its function in our lives is similar to the rudder of a ship. It can lead us in the right direction and help us stay the course. It can guide us to reach a potential that would never be gained without it. It is a key factor in success, faith, good life and good relationships. It has more to do with finding the joy of life than it does with happiness, because happiness depends on "happenings." Joy is a choice we make, and we can choose it regardless of the "happenings" or circumstances of our life.

The problem with changing our attitudes is that for most of us they have become part of our unconscious makeup. We don't consciously spend our whole day humming a negative tune or reciting negative messages to ourselves. However, our unconscious minds eventually come to believe whatever negative spin we have reinforced in ourselves. Eventually it doesn't matter whether we *think* it or not. We believe it.

For years, I drummed my fingers whenever I was waiting, and I didn't realize that I drummed in a recurring pattern or rhythm. One day my husband said to me, "Do you know what you are drumming?" Vapidly I said, "I'm not drumming anything." He said, "Yes, you are. It's the military funeral cadence; you know, what the drummers play during a funeral march." I looked down at my fingers like they had a life of their own. I dared to move them as I had been doing and couldn't believe what I heard. It was the rhythm of the funeral cadence. What kind of a message is that?

It's almost like we have lots of negative attitudes sitting around in our unconscious minds on pilot lights. I think that we then ignite them into thoughts many times during the day: when we look in the mirror and see only our flaws, start a new project and feel overwhelmed, or don't call someone for fear of saying the wrong thing. I evidently felt that life was taking me down a long, dark road of one funeral after another until I miserably came to my own. I had to make a conscious effort to put out that attitude, but I could do it only when it became conscious.

Tim Hansel said in his book, *You Gotta Keep Dancin',* that "pain is inevitable, but misery is optional." Regardless of our circumstances, we can choose any attitude we want. No one can make us have a bad attitude or a good one. We alone can choose. If we believe we are going to be miserable for the rest of our lives, the chances are great that we will be. In grief work the same is true. If we believe that our grief will kill us, we probably will die with a broken heart. If we believe that we can work through the pain and heartache of our losses, we have all we need to do so. If we dare to have hope, our lives will brighten. If we have confidence in doing this hard work, we will be able to help others. The neat thing about attitudes is that they are "catching." So, choose well.

Fifth Team-Training Session:

REDEEMING loss through positive acts of love and service instead of self-defeating reactions

A few weeks after the shooting at Columbine High School, I appeared on *Court TV* in New York City and was asked what I would do with the school if I were the principal there. I told them that I would recommend removing the floor/ceiling between the cafeteria and library and turning that section of the building into a two-story atrium filled with plants. Then I would build a mezzanine around the wall of what is now the library, so a student could still access the books on the walls and sit at tables and smell the air now rich with life-giving oxygen from the plants. I also said that when the contractors had built new walls, I would invite students to come in and paint. In so doing, they would be a part of the rebuilding of their school. Brass nameplates could be affixed to those walls with names of their friends who had died. I mentioned the idea of individual memorial sites on the campus with benches and trees and places to leave messages. I thought the idea of including students in the work of reconstruction would give them an intentional act of remembering and redeeming their losses. To redeem a loss is to trade in some of the pain for something of value, much like we redeem a coupon. The value in this story could be twofold: actual reconstruction and a tangible remembrance for the friends who died there.

I also thought that boxes for donations could be placed in

high school offices across the country, so students everywhere could contribute and become a part of the redemption and remembrance. The value here is helping others. The amazing part of redeeming a loss is that those who engage in the activities report an easing of their longing and a finding of insight about how to be comfortable with that which historically has made us all uncomfortable. Don't forget that "comfort" and "comfortable" are derivations of the same root word, which means to strengthen and soothe and give a new sense of ease. We don't always make that connection, and it is an important one.

An effective way for members of the team to help students understand the connection between engaging in a redeeming activity and processing their own grief is to prepare some ideas and opportunities for them in the aftermath of their losses.

ACTIVITY: GENERATE LIST OF WAYS TO REDEEM A LOSS

Here again you will need a leader for this activity who can encourage and organize participants' input. Generate a list of ways to redeem a loss. You can start with identifying some of the specific losses your school community has faced or is confronting now. You can also use the list of losses generated in the first training session. Work together in groups of two or three to come up with some ideas. Create a list of activities and projects that could be initiated that would relate to the losses. One of the ways I have worked to redeem my losses is by helping other people with their grief. Another way was that I tried to become the kind of teacher my husband was: a champion of underdogs, a compassionate coach, a dedicated worker, etc.

An example of a redemptive act might be that if a student killed in a car wreck was on the track team, his class might sponsor an annual fund-raising 5K race in his name and donate the proceeds to a scholarship fund. The key to this work is similar to remembering; it must be consciously connected to the loss. The runners could wear T-shirts or ribbons with their friend's name on them.

This list of ideas you make will be something you will draw from when you are trying to give ideas to students who get "stuck" in their grief. After you make your list, read the following letter written to Mandy Jackson's parents from their daughter's friend Jason, three years after her death. The work he did redeeming his loss was not specifically connected to Mandy, but he made it so, by doing it in her honor. This example of redeeming a loss is one that students will be able to relate to, even if they are not involved in sports.

Hi Jacksons,

I hope that this letter finds all of you doing well. I am sure that you are keeping busy, and enjoying the beginning of what, hopefully, will be a beautiful fall.

Your daughter was one of the most important people in my life. She taught me so many lessons that I use every day. She taught me how to smile, how to laugh and, most importantly, how to listen. I keep a picture of her in my room, along with a letter she wrote and a lucky penny she gave me. There isn't a day that goes by that I don't remember her and smile.

Two and a half years ago, when Mandy passed away, I didn't know how to act. I had never been faced with something like that before. Even though I was hurting on the inside as much, if not more, than everybody else, I cried very little. I felt like the best way I could help was to be strong for other people to lean on. During that time, though, I did a lot of thinking and came up with my own special way to honor my friend's memory. I decided that the first touchdown I scored at the University of Illinois would be for her.

The first season passed, and the team didn't do very well. In fact, we didn't win a game. I caught my share of passes, but none of them in the end zone. My friend's memory was still fresh in my mind. My second season came and went, and though the team did a little better, I still did not score. But, I remembered my promise. Now, my third season has come around, and it looks like Illinois may have a new team. We won the first two games we played handily. In the second game, against San Diego State, as I was running across the back of the end zone, the ball was suddenly headed in my direction. As if in slow motion, the ball settled into my hands, and I had my first collegiate touchdown.

I didn't hear the roar of the crowd or the shouts of my team-mates. Your daughter's smiling face appeared quietly in my mind. I let out a relieved shout, looked skyward and thrust a finger toward the heavens. But I wasn't celebrating. I was simply talking to an old friend, one that I had made a promise to a long, long time ago. That one was for Mandy.

God bless you all, Jason

The act of redeeming leads us to help others redeem their losses, and this can be a double comfort if we allow ourselves to share it together. Then we can help each other push through the cultural barriers that have conditioned us to think that all grief work should be kept private.

Remembering, however, usually brings up emotions, and we then need to find ways to understand and be comfortable with them. Finding ways to redeem a loss helps us feel stronger because we "did something" to translate our grief into a positive act. And, when we feel stronger, a degree of healing comes.

Sixth Team-Training Session:

UNDERSTANDING and handling emotions

While we all understand the difference between those of us who are controlled more by the heart than the mind and vice versa, everyone lives out lives, careers and relationships based on feelings. If we make life choices based on pragmatic, unemotional, mental calculations that are completely contrary to our feelings, we are still making decisions based on feelings, in this case in opposition to feelings. If we suppress our feelings and pretend they play no vital role in our lives, that takes tremendous energy and concentration. So once again, we are making decisions based on feelings, or the repression of them. If we choose and decide based solely on feeling or find a balance between the heart and the head, feelings are still central to our lives.

Grief is one of the most powerful experiences I have ever encountered. The feelings that accompany it can be overwhelming. Perhaps that is why it is so scary and why we avoid it like the plague. Overpowering emotions keep us from being in control, and control is a highly prized value in our culture. We also live in a quick-fix, hyper-timed, self-help society that is not as comfortable with powerful emotions as it is with powerful mental processes.

I have yet to meet the person who has successfully "thought" his or her way out of grief, but I have met many who have tried. This dilemma of issuing control over our lives between feeling and thinking has become the model for our young people. When working with children, be they in grade school or high school, remember that they have been taught about feelings, mostly by adults in their world and by TV. They have pretty definite ideas by the time they are in the primary grades on what they should or should not feel. They will test everyone around them from time to time to see if their readings are accurate. Then they will gravitate to the people who they cannot read, to more closely examine them.

Kids also have good "guts" or antennae and are accustomed to watching closely what adults do and say, and are especially attentive to nuances. They know when their parents don't like their teachers, which sets up a whole series of conflicting feelings. They know what behaviors their parents dislike in others. They know that the expressions of feelings allowed for men are different from those for women and struggle to get it right. They know what big boys and big girls are supposed to do to control their feelings, which sets up a self-esteem storm when they cannot measure up. They see which expressions of feelings get positive and negative responses and work hard to get the positive strokes we all need. So is it a surprise to any of us that when children act out their feelings, it is not always an accurate

reflection of what is going on inside of them? The one thing
we can know for sure is that things are seldom the way they
seem in the feelings department for children. So we have to
find the Rosetta Stone for feelings in order to interpret what
we hear and see.

The common confusion is that these powerful emotions
do not always present themselves clearly but are encoded in
the behavior of the children. And further, they differ in their
manifestation from one age to another. How does anger
appear in an eighth-grader? What is sadness for a kindergarten girl? How might guilt be seen in a tenth-grade boy?
What about regret or fear for a second-grader? Most educators have insight into these matters but rarely take the
time to sit down and deconstruct them systematically.

An effective way to raise your awareness about complex
emotions after loss is to share and articulate the knowledge
accumulated by the staff experiences.

ACTIVITY: GENERATE LIST OF EMOTIONS AND THEIR MEANING

The leader for this activity should encourage and organize participants' input as they generate a list all of the feelings that are considered normal, natural and even
predictable responses to loss. Once the list is completed,
define them. Even if you are aware of the list of definitions
of emotions in Part IV, Section D, resist going to them for
the purposes of this exercise. Put these emotional descrip-
tors into your own common, everyday language. In so
doing, you will begin to develop your own vocabulary for
explaining emotions to students. It might also be helpful
with a larger team to break up into groups of two or three

and define each emotional response, using language your students will understand. Then come back together as a group and try to decide on some degree of consensus on the definitions. This process will equip you with helpful explanations for students when asked about their feelings.

Next, make a list of good emotions and bad feelings, healthy feelings and unhealthy ones. Now I know what you are thinking: "There are no good or bad feelings, feelings are feelings." Right? Well, of course, you are bright, educated people and you know that is true: Feelings are feelings. They just "are," neither good nor bad, right nor wrong, healthy nor unhealthy. But if this is true, why do we hear some people say, "You shouldn't feel that way"? While we may know the truth, some social mores or cultural opinions say something else, like "anger is bad" and "wanting revenge is unhealthy." So review your list of feelings and decide what the prevailing opinion is about each.

Additional Thoughts

Irritation is a common expression among students, and so are frustration and exasperation. This makes sense because students are in a learning environment, always pressing on to the next skill once the immediate is mastered. So one continuing lesson on feelings in school is handling failure, learning from mistakes and developing self-esteem where it is evident we don't "know it all."

We all, and children in particular, get highly selective about what we "see and hear" when emotions are running rampant. A highly charged set of feelings changes perception of reality. One nasty comment from a classmate can send students home saying, "Everyone hates me."

First Public Meeting

This meeting should include the members of the team and be open to school administrators, teachers, special services personnel and other interested community individuals, especially parents. The reason for including all of these people is for a sharing of information about the team and the purpose of this work in the school district. Prior to this meeting a spokesperson should be chosen. This individual could be the team leader, the organizer of the effort, or someone who has read the book and has strong communications skills. We call this meeting knowing that all attending and involved in the project hope there will never be a need for the team's interventions, but the realities of life in our society indicate, in fact, that the need is pervasive.

A handout should be prepared in advance that contains an overview of this effort to provide assistance to students in learning to deal with loss and grief. A sample of this handout is in Part IV, Section B. This information also is available on the Internet at *www.kidsgrieve.org* as a template designed to be adapted by the school with your own letterhead, team members' names and other community-specific information.

The focus of the meeting will be a sharing of recent findings in the area of grief and the struggles that children have coping with the losses in their lives and school communities. The purpose of the meeting is informational to let all concerned individuals know about the team's existence, training and willingness to help students when the need arises. It is important to explain that this endeavor is one of support and information-sharing, not therapy. There will not be organized group meetings but rather a team of people available to students. If at some time a support group forms, that is fine, but initially the team is training to be "on call" to assist students as they work out ways to cope and live with life-changing losses. The work will be done on an individual or small-group basis and is mostly confidential. I say "mostly" because it is important to include a student's family in any part or the entire endeavor, and confidentiality is never appropriate when you fear for a student's safety or health. However, the work is confidential in the interaction. Team members will respect confidentially shared conversations with students and will not divulge that information to other students or teachers without the expressed consent of the student.

Another important issue in this meeting is communication. Since this work will be adopted and adapted by the school system, it will develop and expand according to the needs of the district, the creativity of the team and the input of the community. We want people to know that the team exists and the names of its members. As people share this information with each other, the likelihood of using the team's resources will increase. What this book gives everyone is the structure and some guidelines. As this area of intervention grows over the coming years and new research is conducted, the shape and content of this work will change. It is not the intent of *Mourning and Dancing for Schools* and the resulting programs to propose solutions to our nation's problems with violence, murder, "accidents," gun control, hatred and isolation. This is grief work, and it takes place in the aftermath of death and other traumatic losses. However, I think these interventions may have a positive reverse effect and potentially prevent the violent impulse. If we begin to have conversations and intentional interactions to process grief, if people share honestly the impact loss has on our lives (sometimes over a lifetime), perhaps we can reduce the incidence of hatred, violence or murder. If students have an outlet for the pain that may lead to acting out and a vehicle for understanding their emotions, the result may be a reduction in frustration and the urge for revenge.

A format that can be used for the public meeting is a panel presentation. The team could sit at a table in the theater or all-purpose room and have a couple of people share the purpose and direction of the endeavor. This format also gives the community a chance to feel familiar with the team members, in order to make a referral. Of most importance, this meeting needs to point out that our society will likely continue on its whirlwind pace in dealing with life, including its problems. This fast-paced approach to getting us fixed, healed, recovered, renewed or replaced has not been successful in the area of grief. It will be helpful to explain that people grieve over time but not all of the time. People want to know that others know that their lives have been radically changed, in some cases forever, and that it takes time and support to adjust to those changes. This meeting and the question/answer session that follows provide opportunity for communication for everyone involved. A suggestion box or an email address should be made available for people to communicate their ideas and support with the school team.

Part IV

Resources

This resource section is designed to be a work in process. It is a beginning for this endeavor of helping ourselves and others do the intentional work of grieving. The worksheets and bibliography are available on the Web site in template form, so they can be personalized and downloaded for use by a team or personally by individuals. See *www.kidsgrieve.org*.

Section A: Articles

Publicity is a sensitive issue when dealing with loss and grieving people and must be handled with respect for the individuals involved in the loss. The more information available to catch the public eye, however, the greater the awareness for understanding the realities of loss in our lives and the need for grief support endeavors.

"Hurrying Healing," by Ellen Goodman, *Boston Globe*, 1998

"An August of Discontent," by Sally Downham Miller, *Journal and Courier*, 1997

"Mandy's Friends Learn How to Cope with Grief," by Michelle Falardeau, *Journal and Courier*, 1997

Section B: Team-Training Worksheets

The worksheets included here are also available in template form on the Web site *www.kidsgrieve.org.* They can serve as discussion guides for learning about healthy grieving, for training a support team or for keeping a personal journal.

- Training-Session Worksheets
- Additional Team-Training Topics
- Introductory Workshop on Grief and Loss Work in Schools
- Agenda for a Public Meeting
- Packet of Information Sent to Teachers and Parents in Waldwick, N.J.

Section C: Books, Videos, Organizations and Reviews

This section will grow as our cultural awareness grows regarding "what helps." The Web site will provide a place where individuals or schools can submit book reviews and critiques of materials.

- Bibliography
- Reviews

Section D: Additional Information

- Definitions of Emotional Responses
- Understanding the Role of Emotions in Grief
- Understanding Anger

Section E: Writing Through the Storm

Letters and other messages written by grieving individuals are tangible expressions of love and remembrance that can be saved and reread.

Section A: Articles

Hurrying Healing
by Ellen Goodman
Boston Globe, January 6, 1998

I don't remember when the words first began to echo in the hollow aftermath of loss. But now it seems that every public or private death, every moment of mourning is followed by a call for "healing," a cry for "closure."

Last month, driving home in my car just 24 hours after three Kentucky students were shot to death in a school prayer meeting, I heard a Paducah minister talk about healing. The three teenagers had yet to be buried, and he said it was time to begin the healing process, as if there were an antibiotic to be applied at the first sign of pain among the survivors.

Weeks later, at a Christmas party, a man offered up a worried sigh about a widowed mutual friend. "It's been two years," he said, "and she still hasn't achieved closure." The words pegged her as an underachiever who failed the required course in Mourning 201, who wouldn't graduate with her grief class.

This vocabulary of "healing" and "closure" has spread across the post-mortem landscape like a nail across my blackboard. It comes with an intonation of sympathy but an accent of impatience. It suggests, after all, that death is something to be dealt with, that loss is something to get over—according to a prescribed emotional timetable.

It happened again when the Terry Nichols verdict came down. No sooner had the mixed counts of guilty and innocent been announced than the usually jargon-free Peter

Jennings asked how it would help the "healing" for Oklahoma City. Assorted commentators and reporters asked the families whether they felt a sense of "closure."

The implicit expectation, even demand, was that the survivors of 168 deaths would traverse a similar emotional terrain and come to the finish line at the same designated time. Were two and a half years too long to mourn a child blown up in a building?

It was the families themselves who set us straight with responses as personal and diverse as one young mother who said, "It's time to move on," and another who described her heart this way: "Sometimes I feel like it's bleeding." In the Nichols sentencing trial last week, we got another rare sampling of raw grief. Laura Kennedy testified that in the wake of her son's death in 1995, "I have an emptiness inside of me that's there all the time." Diane Leonard said that since her husband's death her life "has a huge hole that can't be mended."

By the second day, however, the cameras had turned away, the microphones had turned a deaf ear, as if they had heard enough keening. Again, observers asked what affect a life-or-death sentence would have on, of course, "healing" and "closure."

I do not mean to suggest that the people who testified were "typical" mourners or the Oklahoma bombing a "typical" way of death. I mean to suggest that grief is always atypical—as individual as the death and the mourner.

The American way of dealing with it however has turned grieving into a set process with rules, stages, and of course deadlines. We have, in essence, tried to make a science of grief, to tuck messy emotions under neat clinical labels— like "survivor guilt" or "detachment."

Sometimes, we confuse sadness with depression, replace comfort with Prozac. We expect, maybe insist upon an end to grief. Trauma, pain, detachment, acceptance in a year— time's up.

But in real lives, grief is a train that doesn't run on anyone else's schedule. Jimmie Holland at New York's Sloan-Kettering Hospital, who has studied the subject, knows that "normal grief may often be an ongoing lifelong process." Indeed, she says, "The expectation of healing becomes an added burden. We create a sense of failure. We hear people say, 'I can't seem to reach closure, I'm not doing it fast enough.'"

Surely it is our own anxiety in the presence of pain, our own fear of loss and death, that makes us wish away another's grief or hide our own. But in every life, losses will accumulate like stones in a backpack. We will all be caught at times between remembrance and resilience.

So whatever our national passion for emotional efficiency, for quality-time parents and one-minute managers, there simply are no one-minute mourners. Hearts heal faster from surgery than from loss. And when the center of someone's life has been blown out like the core of a building, is it any wonder if it takes so long even to find a door to close?

An August of Discontent
by Dr. Sally Downham Miller
Journal and Courier, Lafayette, Indiana,
August 25, 1997

It's August, full of back-to-school readiness, preparations for new beginnings, clean slates and fresh starts. So why are we sad? Okay, the summer is over, but it's more than that. Something else has robbed us of the excitement and expectations for the new school year, the fall season. Perhaps, we are grieving. Maybe we have seen too many dreams snuffed out this summer, and we are hesitant to envision good things coming. Maybe we are waiting for the other shoe to drop. We have been through quite a lot since we first heard of Columbine High School, the bells tolling again in Camelot, the storms devastating homes across our country, and a gunman shooting down our babies again, this time in L.A. Now, we are sick at heart as we watch families like ours try to move brick and mortar off of their homes and loved ones in Turkey, with wooden sticks and handmade pulleys. We have plenty of reasons to feel sad, and a present sadness has a way of connecting us to the losses of our lives.

As a young wife and mother in the *Father Knows Best* era, I believed in the ultimate good in life. My Prince Charming had swooped down and carried me away on the back of his athletic scholarship to a land of college classes and dreams of the ways we would change the world for the good, especially for the good of children. We didn't mind sacrificing. We had each other and the promise of America in our hip pocket. If we just held onto the dream and worked hard it would all unfold as surely as the sun would come out. I even took in ironing to help make ends meet. For my birthday, my husband bought me a little silver iron for my charm bracelet. Not so glamorous, but we were building up riches of another kind, investing in the kingdom of hope and prosperity and strong families. And we weren't alone. Others were following this dream too, and together we played cards on Saturday nights and nursed our babies and talked about what we would do when we had money.

Then August came and the dreams of our kingdom crumbled nine days after my husband, Bob, received a cancer diagnosis at age twenty-four. I walked out of a hospital in Indianapolis a widow with vivid testimony that dreams don't come true. I was glad I had never told anybody I had secretly believed it was true for us. How naive! I began the isolating process of running through the only maze of grief our society had laid out for us, the maze of getting over it and going on and finding closure. I listened to messages like crying only makes you feel worse and talking about it doesn't change anything. I tried to put together a new life and it felt like empty motions. I tried to make my children my reason for living. But, I didn't want to grieve. That felt overwhelming, too powerful to control, too upsetting. So, I put it away in the dungeon of my heart and the years passed by.

Unresolved grief, however, needs to find its resolve. It will take any escape route it can find out of the deep recesses to which we have banished it. The reason it catches us off guard is that we have believed this is possible. We have believed the repressive messages of our quick cure, hyper-timed, self-help society. We think that if we develop the right habits, take the right vitamins, think the right thoughts and exercise we can overcome anything, maybe even death. Then when a word or an anniversary or the subtlety of a scent reminds us, up it all comes out of the depths, and we scramble to push it back down again, wondering where we failed. Wondering what is wrong with us.

One of the best expressions of unresolved grief I have ever seen was at Diana Spencer's funeral. We huddled over our coffee cups in the dark hours before dawn that morning, sensing our connection to each other, but thankful to be alone. Alone to cry without needing to explain. Alone to remember that of which, perhaps, we have never spoken. But it has always been there with us. Sometimes silent for years, but never gone. Amazed every time we remember that it can feel so current, as though it only happened yesterday. Watching the funeral we let the music of the dirge fill our souls and the rituals express our sorrow, both touching places where words cannot reach. We allowed the specter of ceremony to draw us in. We let the Earl of Spencer express our anger and felt satisfaction in the eloquent vehemence of his eulogy. We watched her sons and ached for the times our children and we have felt abandoned. We looked at her husband and prayed that our sons would become princes who would never betray their trust. We re-felt the days when the dreams and people in our lives died.

Now, as the August anniversary of that loss comes around, we have endured yet another fairytale tragedy in the Kennedy family. And we felt it all so powerfully. We watched the empty water for hours on end, not wanting to give up: hoping, praying, cursing, and wanting the inevitable not to be so. Even conspiracy theories and dreams of Robinson Crusoe tempted us. *Maybe they had become so sick of the public prying and the paparazzi following, that they planned an escape. Maybe there was a boat nearby and they parachuted out of the plane and were picked up and spirited away to Shangri la or Camelot. Maybe the mist of Martha's Vineyard was the perfect cover. Maybe they are safe.* But inside of ourselves we knew differently, and all too soon their deaths were confirmed.

Now the Kennedy tragedy is woven in with the images of students returning to Columbine High School, and toddlers being led out of another bloody school in L.A. No wonder it is has become commonplace for these losses to take up space in our conscious and unconscious minds, leaving a malaise of sadness on our nation. We have tried to refocus and put it away, but it seems to have wangled its way into the corners of our hearts and souls. While grieving as a nation is more symbolic than personal, we know that the grieving for the families is firsthand and deeply personal, and it is this difference that both connects us and separates us. The deaths of Diana Spencer, the Kennedys and all of the children who died this year are tragic and senseless losses, but the tears that were cried, the grief shared, the flowers laid were not only for them. They were for all of our losses: deaths, marriages, wayward children, health, jobs, dreams, hopes. The power of our own grief, some of which we have worked many years to hide, contributes greatly to what we have been feeling. So we ache for the families we have watched on TV, as we do for our own loves and losses that others have insisted we should "be over by now."

Perhaps, as a nation, we need to endorse and allow times and places and ceremonies and opportunities to process our losses, so we can live with them, rather than run from or deny them. I wonder what would happen if in all of our hometowns we had remembrance services annually to process our grief, or remembrance gardens where we could dig and plant new life, or centers for loss and grief where people could go and find comfort and nurturing contact with others? I think we need to change our social mores about grief and help people deal with it. This is the way I have learned to resolve my losses. By running support groups, teaching seminars, training school teams and writing books I am redeeming my loss into something of great value, both to keep and to share with others. These are my dreams this August, and I am working on them.

Mandy's Friends Learn
How to Cope with Grief
by Michelle Falardeau
Journal and Courier, Lafayette, Indiana, May 1997

In the week since Amanda Jackson's life was cut short, her friends have done much to keep her memory alive. They have planted a pear tree, circled by daisies. They have painted a barn. They have laughed. They have cried.

Jackson, eighteen, died a week ago today when her car was struck by two trains at the Norfolk Southern railway crossing on Greenbush Street. Since then, her friends, many of whom graduated with "Mandy" from Harrison High School the week before, have begun the first stages of healing. On Thursday, about fifty friends and their parents met at the high school for a session on helping the healing process continue. They learned from someone who has been there, Dr. Sally Downham Miller, that planting trees and painting barns is a good place to start.

"If you put the grief inside, if you stuff it, if you pretend it isn't there, it grows," she said. "Pretty soon it takes more energy to stuff it than it does to live."

Miller, whose first husband died at twenty-four, just nine days after he was diagnosed with cancer, offered friends and family the hope of healing.

"If you are willing to be in touch with the pain, if you are willing to work that through, there is healing available," she said.

Part of the grieving process includes remembering, even memorializing Amanda, she said. In the past week, some have painted personal notes on the side of a farmer's barn near her high school. Messages such as: "We love you Mandy J. You complete us."

Miller commended them for their actions.

"The healthiest thing you could do is your barn," she said. "Someone asked if that was a good thing to do. Yes. Every time you do something to remember, you are putting all the parts back together again."

Laurie Baker and Kristen Stein attended, looking for answers. Baker, a classmate, said she has cried and laughed and stayed close to friends. And she and others planted a pear tree surrounded by daisies, Amanda's favorite flower. "The tree is in her front yard, right outside her window. The leaves will turn purple in the fall. She loved that color. In spring, it will have white blossoms. And it's a teardrop shape."

Miller told the crowd that there would always be a hole in their hearts where Amanda once was. "Our job is not to get over it, but to learn to live with it. Going on with our lives does not mean leaving her behind but, rather, incorporating the best of Amanda into your life. Remembering, crying, feeling — it is the way to heal."

One friend said she might get a tattoo to remember her friend. Miller suggested a heart and a daisy. "Just a suggestion," she said as a circle of laughter bubbled up.

She encouraged the young people to weave the best qualities of their friend into their lives as a living memorial. The friends called out adjectives describing their friend: understanding, funny, honest, intelligent.

"In remembering Mandy, look at yourself and see what isn't like Mandy that you would like to be — become Mandy. Take on the characteristics she valued. Who she was is who you will continue to be."

Baker said she'd do whatever it takes. "Mandy was my best friend," she said. "I will do anything that will help."

THERAPIST: LOOK FOR WARNING SIGNALS

"All too often, teens are drawn to the loved one who has died," says Dr. Sally Downham Miller, a grief therapist. "If the child has been lied to about some aspect of the death or kept from knowing of the loss, outside intervention could be in order to help the child deal with the grief."

Another complication to the grief process: the child, who experienced a difficult relationship with the deceased, Miller says.

Other signs a child might need outside intervention include:

- Pretending absolutely nothing has happened
- Declining interest in schoolwork or developing a phobic fear of school
- Threatening suicide
- Panicking frequently
- Delving into drugs or alcohol use
- Committing serious socially delinquent acts
- Isolating from other children
- Assaulting others frequently or being cruel to animals

The Aftercare Resource Center offers grief support meetings to children, teens and adults, who would like to share their grief, help them learn to live with their grief and to celebrate life as they go forward. For more information, call 765-742-9546.

Section B:
Team-Training Worksheets

First Training-Session Worksheet

Realizing that everyone experiences loss

Generate a list of the family and personal losses that students, teachers and school staff experience.

Example:
Death
   Different types — accident, illness
   Different relationships — parent, friend
Divorce

Second Training-Session Worksheet

Recognizing that grief is a natural human response to loss

Generate a list of the accompanying losses, or "ripple effects" of loss, that students might experience.

Example:
Divorce—loss of home/house, loss of family as we knew it, etc.

Third Training-Session Worksheet

Remembering our losses and how they affect our lives in healthy and unhealthy ways

Generate a list of actions that we can take to help students remember their losses in healthy ways.

Example:
Intentional writing activities; i.e., journal, letters, etc.

Fourth Training-Session Worksheet

Redefining the way we view loss and
its consequences in ourselves and in others

Generate a list of positive and negative reactions that
students might exhibit in response to their losses.

Example:

Negative	*Positive*
Doomed	A survivor
Punished	Having a new understanding

Fifth Training-Session Worksheet

Redeeming loss through positive acts of love and service instead of self-defeating reactions

Generate a list of ideas that students and the school community can undertake to turn their individual and school losses into redeeming acts of love and service.

Sixth Training-Session Worksheet

Emotions

Generate a list of emotional responses to grief.
Once the list is complete, determine how each response
is judged typically in our society, e.g., some are
perceived as positive or healthy and
some are seen as negative and hurtful.

ADDITIONAL TEAM-TRAINING TOPICS

If the team wants to continue their training, the following topics provide some suggestions for doing so:

- Modeling healthy grieving
- Talking to people who do not understand healthy grief
- Becoming comfortable with the emotions that accompany grief
- The expressions and denial of anger
- Understanding guilt, remorse and "what ifs"
- Recognizing red flags for referrals
- How to handle two-minute conferences
- Group vs. individual counseling
- What to say and what not to say
- Setting up after-school support groups
- Remembering and commemorating activities

INTRODUCTORY WORKSHOP ON GRIEF AND LOSS WORK IN SCHOOLS

The purpose of this workshop is to provide an overview of processing grief in schools, as it is important to communicate with our students, parents and community regarding the work we are proposing. In so doing, we hope to gain their support and apprise them of the resources we will provide for our students. While we are reading the overview, a sign-up sheet will be passed around so we know who is in attendance. (The overview can be read aloud and then disseminated or read in small groups by workshop participants, with a few minutes for discussion. Once it is read, a small time [five minutes, suggested] for questions or discussion can be offered.) The time allotted for this workshop is fifty minutes.

OVERVIEW: Crisis management teams have become adept at handling trauma in our schools. The emotional and psychological interventions of these counselors and the teams they assemble are crucial, but the deep healing does not take place in the first few days or even the first few weeks following a crisis or trauma. This is not news to any of us. We know that the imprints left by tragedy, especially in a child's life, are there long after order is restored and the ceremonies have ended. That is when the work of grieving and healing begins. We know that children will continue to experience the effects of loss for years to come, some of them for their lifetime. The topic of "helping people grieve over time," however, does not get the same attention as "dealing with death and crisis" and the immediate aftermath. The work of processing grief over time, in our student's lives, is what we are discussing today.

In order to do this grief work, we are proposing assembling a team of people who want to volunteer their time to be trained and to be available when our students need them. Together they will develop interventions that help children in our school family a week later, four months later, years later. They will promote understanding in our community that some life-changing losses can affect us for the rest of our life, but that does not mean we are doomed to suffer in silence or live out a diminished existence. This work is about hope. The goal will be finding ways to deal with the powerful, passion-filled experiences we know as grief. They will try to help our students:

- to understand the ways young people act out their feelings, be they repressed or expressed in eruptive fits
- to recognize the changes that occur as a result of loss

- to acknowledge the effects of these changes and learn how to manage them
- to find healthy ways to help themselves and others go through grief

The purpose of the training, interventions and ongoing work of a Grief and Loss Team is to help restore health and healing after the counselors brought in during a crisis return to their own jobs. It is not a replacement program for school counselors, nor is it a grief therapy program. It is not a curriculum for teaching death education, nor is it a book about preventing violence or crises in our schools. Inherent in this philosophy, however, is the belief that helping children find ways to live with loss and to work through grief and to have hope can reduce some of the tragedies that occur in our school families.

TRAINING SAMPLE

This exercise will give you a sample of the training experiences our team members will have together, in greater depth.

Exercise #1 — Generate a list of all of the losses we experience in a lifetime.

Assign someone to write on the board as the group brainstorms this list. Accept all contributions without discussion.

Exercise #2 — Using the list from exercise #1, underline three common losses you know of that students experience today. Pick one and make a list of the accompanying losses or changes that occur in the aftermath.

Exercise #3 — Generate a list of all possible reactions to loss, many of which we will refer to as emotional responses.

Again, pick someone to write on the board. Refrain from making comments or having any discussions.

Exercise #4—Generate a list of books, videos, organizations, support groups, or other resources available to you in your community or surrounding area that can assist in this grief recovery work.

Exercise #5—Discuss what you learned from the above. You now have an idea of what the team will be doing. In addition, they will be learning strategies and interventions for helping students, perhaps even starting a support group.

In conclusion, we are sending back around our sign-up sheet so you can check off your name if you want to be contacted when we start our team, so you can participate if you are able at that time. If you are not, please become our goodwill ambassadors and tell people about this valuable effort.

Thank you for coming!

"Grief takeد place over time,
but it ∂oeدn't take place all the time"

Agenda for a Public Meeting
Jefferson High School Auditorium
November 18, 2000 — 7 P.M.

Topic: Grief and Loss Team Presentation

Welcome and Introductions — Team Leader
Board of Education, Superintendent, Principals and Team Members

Purpose — The Grief and Loss Team would like to inform you of our existence and our work. We began training together in August to find ways to help our students process grief in the weeks, months and years following a loss or trauma. This work takes place after the crisis management team has finished their work in the first days after a crisis occurs. We understand that students who have suffered a life-changing loss will not "get over it" when the ceremonies have ended, and we want to be available to help them when their grief comes up over time.

Presentation — Team Members
Different members of the team will explain the work we are doing. The first person, John Doe, will tell you about our training. Then Sue Smith will tell you about our planned interventions.

Questions and Answers — Team Leader
We both desire and need your support, so please ask any questions you may have or share with us any suggestions you may have.

Packet of Information Sent to Teachers and Parents in Waldwick, New Jersey

The following letters and information constitute the packet we sent to teachers and parents in the Waldwick, N. J., School System when Carolyn Small, school principal, died. The template for this information was drawn from *Sudden Death: Crisis in the School* by Louise Aldrich and reprinted as they were used by her permission.

October 12, 1999

Dear Parents:

We were recently saddened in our educational community by the sudden death of Mrs. Carolyn Small, Principal of Traphagen School. As a school community, we express our condolences to the family and friends of Mrs. Small.

Often when we hear of another's death, our own feelings about death surface. Children, like adults, begin to think of their own death, and many normal feelings surface. These feelings may focus on the person who had died, another person who has died in the past, an impending death, or anxiety about death in general.

As a school staff member we encourage you to listen carefully to your child, answering questions openly and honestly if they occur, and letting children know that even adults don't have all the answers concerning questions about death.

Accepting your child's feelings and validating these feelings are beneficial. During these weeks and months ahead, confusing feelings may surface periodically, and it is helpful to discuss them with an adult.

Counselors from our schools and community mental health professionals have been available all day today, if the students chose to talk with one. Counselors will again be present in the school on Thursday. All schools will be closed on Wednesday, the day of Mrs. Small's funeral. Schools will be in session on Monday, October 25. Parent conferences will be rescheduled.

As a school, our focus is on the living. As adults we can help facilitate the possible feelings of our children concerning this death. Dr. Downham is available at the Traphagen School and can assist you in this area, if any questions arise. Please feel free to call me also, if you have any concerns.

The wake for Mrs. Small will be held at the Vander Platt Funeral Home on Godwin Avenue in Wyckoff from 2:00–4:00 P.M. and 7:00–9:00 P.M. on Tuesday, October 12. A funeral mass will be celebrated at 10:00 A.M. on Wednesday at St. Elizabeth's R.C. Church in Wyckoff. In lieu of flowers the family has asked that donations be sent to the Traphagen School.

Sincerely,
John J. Szabo, Ed.D., Superintendent

INFORMATION REGARDING MRS. SMALL

Information for Teachers

According to Denise Ponte, Carolyn's friend, on Saturday Carolyn went to a wedding. Later in the evening Carolyn went to BJ's. She was alone in the Expedition van/truck. After shopping, she took Route 23 North to Route 287 North. Near to that intersection, Carolyn saw an accident happening in the right lane. She tried to avoid the accident by veering left but one car from the accident shot across 287 and broadsided her on the passenger side, ejecting Carolyn. The van rolled over three times. She died instantly.

Information for Students

I have some news to tell you. As some of you may have already heard, Mrs. Small died in a car accident on Saturday night. This is a very sad time for all of us who knew Mrs. Small.

Probably some of you had the opportunity to discuss this with your families. (Here, ask who heard the news of Mrs. Small's death over the weekend, what they heard, etc. You want to give the children an opportunity to share what they heard, dispel rumors and ask questions.)

You might be feeling sad, confused or afraid. You also may be feeling no different than you usually do. You may not feel sad until later. There are helping people in the library today if you feel the need to share your feelings.

(Now offer the children a chance to make a card to send to Mrs. Small's family, write a poem or draw a picture about Mrs. Small.)

Suggestions to School Personnel, in Order to Facilitate Students' Grief:

- Acknowledge the death; do not pretend life is unchanged
- Tell the children the truth
- Role model grief
- Communicate what is normal in grieving
- Accept another's feelings and know everyone has their own way and time to grieve
- Support in a nonjudgmental manner without assuming anything
- Nurture without intruding on a student's or staff member's privacy
- Allow yourself to discuss the death with peers and family, and how the death/deaths have affected you personally

Developmental Ages and Possible Reactions to Death

AGE	THINK	FEEL	DO
3–5 Years	• Death is temporary & reversible • Finality of death is not evident • Death mixed up with trips, sleep • May wonder what deceased is doing	• Sad • Anxious • Withdrawn • Confused about changes • Angry • Scared • Cranky (feelings are acted out in play)	• Cry • Fight • Are interested in dead things • Acts as if death never happened
6–9 Years	• About the finality of death • About the biological processes of death • Death is related to mutilation • A spirit gets you when you die • About who will care for them if a parent dies • Their actions and words caused the death	• Sad • Anxious • Withdrawn • Confused about changes • Angry • Scared • Cranky (feelings are acted out in play)	• Behave aggressively • Behave withdrawn • Experience nightmares • Act as if death never happened • Lack concentration • Have a decline in grades

AGE	THINK	FEEL	DO
9–12 Years	• About and understand the finality of death • Death is hard to talk about • That death may happen again, and feel anxious • About death with jocularity • About what will happen if their parent(s) die • Their actions and words caused the death	• Vulnerable • Anxious • Scared • Lonely • Confused • Angry • Sad • Abandoned • Guilty • Fearful • Worried • Isolated	• Behave aggressively • Behave withdrawn • Talk about physical aspects of death • Act like it never happened, not show feelings • Experience nightmares • Lack concentration • Have a decline in grades
12 Years and Up (Teenagers)	• About and understand the finality of death • If they show their feelings they will be weak • They need to be in control of their feelings • About death with jocularity • Only about life before or after the death • Their actions and words caused the death	• Vulnerable • Anxious • Scared • Lonely • Confused • Angry • Sad • Abandoned • Guilty • Fearful • Worried • Isolated	• Behave impulsively • Argue, scream, fight • Allow themselves to be in dangerous situations • Grieve for what might have been • Experience nightmares • Act like it never happened • Lack concentration • Have a decline in grades

Reprinted with permission from *Sudden Death: Crisis in the School*, by Louise Aldrich, MSW, LCSW.

Some of the normal feelings that will be expressed are:

SAD: Some children/adolescents may cry a lot to express sadness.

HAPPY: Children and adolescents often respond to death in a joking manner. When first hearing the news, they may snicker or laugh out loud. This response is in disbelief of the occurrence, and children and adolescents may respond with the opposite feeling that you would anticipate.

ANGRY: Many youngsters are very angry when a classmate or a teacher dies. They may respond verbally, but in many children their behavior is indicative of their affect and they respond in a hostile manner. Acting on that anger is not acceptable. A concern for school personnel is aggression.

SHOCKED: Many young people may be in a state of disbelief and can have physical symptoms that relate to their shock. Vomiting, shivering, wetting themselves and crying may be some of the physical symptoms that you may encounter.

GUILTY: Guilt is a familiar feeling that relates to magical thinking. One may think that he or she was able to stop the course of life events because he or she did or did not do something. It is a universal feeling and only time and reason help it dissipate.

ABANDONED: Young people may feel insecure and alone without their deceased friend or teacher, and feel as though they have been abandoned by them.

ANXIOUS: Many youngsters think that another death may happen to either their friends or their family. If a child died in a traffic accident, others may be fearful of traveling on the same street, or if a child died of an illness, there may be fear that one will contract the same illness.

WORRIED: Children and adolescents worry whether they will die. If a student dies, other students may worry about their own death.

DIFFERENT: Frequently, children and adolescents feel that they are different from those who have not experienced a death, and thus choose to isolate themselves from others.

OVERWHELMED: Young people who have experienced a death may feel upset or overwhelmed in many areas. They may feel stressed in their school performance because it is too difficult to concentrate, or they may feel overwhelmed and devastated because death is so difficult to sort out without support and nurturing.

CONFUSED: Death by its nature is confusing, but when children and adolescents deny its universality, and irreversibility, it is difficult to process. At each developmental stage, young people reprocess the death and learn more about its nature.

Reprinted with permission from *Sudden Death: Crisis in the School,* by Louise Aldrich, MSW, LCSW.

FOLLOW-UP LETTERS:

October 14, 1999

Dear Traphagen Staff:

I know that the past several days have been extremely difficult for you. Dealing with your own grief and loss while attending to the needs of your students requires a degree of professionalism and compassion which transcends your role as classroom teachers.

Please accept my heartfelt thanks for all that you have done in dealing with this tragic loss. I know that Carolyn would have been proud of your efforts.

Sincerely,
John J. Szabo, Superintendent

October 14, 1999

Dear Crisis Management Team:

Words cannot express adequately my deep appreciation of your efforts over the past several days. The sudden loss of Carolyn was an event that could have had a catastrophic impact upon many of our students, had it not been for your professional intervention. Your kindness, compassion and guidance assisted our entire community through a very difficult time of shock and grief.

I thank you for your efforts on behalf of our educational community. I know that Carolyn would have been pleased and proud of all that you have done.

Sincerely,
John J. Szabo, Superintendent

Letters personalized from templates provided in *Sudden Death: Crisis in the School*, by Louise Aldrich, MSW, LCSW.

Section C:
Books, Videos, Organizations
and Reviews

Bibliography

JUVENILE

Brown, Marc. *When Dinosaurs Die: A Guide to Understanding Death.* New York: Little, Brown & Co., 1998.

Buscaglia, Leo F. *The Fall of Freddie the Leaf.* Austin, Texas: Holt, Rinehart & Winston, 1983.

Cave, Anne Good, and Janice Skivington. *Balloons for Trevor: Understanding Death.* St. Louis, Mo.: Concordia Publishing House, 1998.

Cohen, Cindy Klein, John T. Heiney, and Michael J. Gordon. *Daddy's Promise.* Bloomfield Hills, Mich.: Promise Publications, 1997.

Johnston, Marianne. *When Your Pet Dies.* New York: Rosen Publishing Group, 1997.

Kent, Jack. *There's No Such Thing as a Dragon.* New York: Scholastic Press, 1975.

Mundy, Michaeline. *Sad Isn't Bad: A Good-Grief Guidebook for Kids Dealing with Loss.* Saint Meinrad, Ind.: Abbey Press, 1998.

Silverman, Janis. *Help Me Say Goodbye: Activities for Helping Children Cope When a Special Person Dies.* Minneapolis, Minn.: Fairview Press, 1998.

Simon, Norma. *The Saddest Time.* New York: Albert Whitman & Co., 1986.

Varley, Susan. *Badger's Parting Gifts.* New York: Mulberry Books, 1992.

Viorst, Judith. *The Tenth Good Thing About Barney.* New York: Aladdin Paperbacks, 1976.

Weitzman, Elizabeth. *When a Parent Dies.* New York: Rosen Publishing Group, 1996.

OLDER JUVENILE

Heegaard, Marge. *When Something Terrible Happens: Children Learn to Cope with Grief.* Minneapolis, Minn.: Woodland Press, 1992.

Palmer, Pat. *I Wish I Could Hold Your Hand: A Child's Guide to Grief and Loss.* San Luis Obispo, Calif.: Impact Publishing Co., 1994.

Shriver, Maria. *What Is Heaven?* New York: Golden Books, 1999.

YOUNG ADULTS

Gootman, Marilyn. *When a Friend Dies: A Book for Teens About Grieving and Healing.* Minneapolis, Minn.: Free Spirit Publishing, 1994.

Grollman, Earl. *Straight Talk About Death for Teenagers: How to Cope with Losing Someone You Love.* Boston, Mass.: Beacon Press, 1993.

Perschy, Mary Kelly. *Helping Teens Through Grief.* Bristol, Penn.: Taylor & Francis, 1997.

Traisman, Enid. *Fire in My Heart, Ice in My Veins: A Journal for Teenagers Experiencing a Loss.* Omaha, Neb.: Centering Corp., 1992.

MULTI-AGED

Canfield, Jack, et al. *Chicken Soup for the Kid's Soul.* Deerfield Beach, Fla.: Health Communications, Inc., 1998.

Johnson, Joy, and Marvin Johnson. *Children Grieve, Too: A Book for Families Who Have Experienced Death.* Omaha, Neb.: Centering Corp, 1998.

Schaefer, Dan, and Christine Lyons. *How Do We Tell Children: A Step by Step Guide for Helping Children Two to Teen When Someone Dies.* New York: Newmarket Press, 1993.

ADULTS

Aldrich, Louise, MSW, LCSW. *Sudden Death: Crisis in the School* (self-published), 1060 Kings Highway North, Cherry Hill, N.J. 08034-1910.

Dayton, Tian. *Heartwounds: The Impact of Unresolved Trauma and Grief on Relationships.* Deerfield Beach, Fla.: Health Communications, Inc., 1997.

Dayton, Tian. *Drama Games: Techniques for Self-Development.* Deerfield Beach, Fla.: Health Communications, Inc., 1990.

Fitzgerald, Helen. *The Grieving Child.* New York: Fireside Press, 1992.

Goodman, Ellen. "Hurrying Healing." *Boston Globe,* 6 June, 1998.

Grant, Julane. *When Your Friend's Child Dies: A Guide to Being a Thoughtful and Caring Friend.* Scappoose, Ore.: Angel Hugs Publishing, 1998.

Grollman, Earl. *Bereaved Children and Teens.* Boston, Mass.: Beacon Press, 1996.

Grollman, Earl, and Susan Avisha. *Talking About Death: A Dialogue Between Parent and Child.* Boston, Mass.: Beacon Press, 1991.

Harris, Janice. *No Time for Good-byes: Coping with Sorrow, Anger and Injustice After a Tragic Death.* Ventura, Calif.: Pathfinders Publisher, 1991.

Huntley, Theresa. *Helping Children Grieve: When Someone They Love Dies.* Minneapolis, Minn.: Augsburg Fortress Publications, 1991.

James, John W., and Russell Friedman. *The Grief Recovery Handbook: The Action Program for Moving Beyond Death, Divorce and Other Losses.* New York: HarperCollins, 1998.

Kubler-Ross, Elisabeth. *On Death and Dying.* New York: Collier Books, 1997.

Lang, Sandi, and Gordon Lang. *Grief's Courageous Journey: A Workbook.* Oakland, Calif.: New Harbinger Press, 1995.

Miller, Sally Downham. *Mourning and Dancing.* Deerfield Beach, Fla.: Health Communications, Inc., 1999.

Warren, Neil. *Make Anger Your Ally.* Dallas, Texas: Word Books, 1990.

Wolfelt, Alan. *Healing the Bereaved Child.* Fort Collins, Colo.: Companion Press, 1996.

VIDEOS

Crenshaw, David. *Grief: How to Help Children Feel, Deal and Heal,* *www.griefsupportvideo.com.*

Marta, Suzy, and Medard Laz. *Rainbows,* *www.rainbows.org* or 1-800-266-3206.

The Fall of Freddie the Leaf, The Felicea Foundation, AIMS Media, Van Nuys, Calif. 91406 or 818-785-4111.

ORGANIZATIONS

Centering Corporation
Joy Johnson, Editor
1531 N. Saddle Creek Road
Omaha, Nebraska 68104-5074

Compassionate Friends
www.compassionatefriends.org or 1-800-807-8357
This is a support organization for parents who lose children.

Survivors of Suicide
www.suicidology.org/survivorssupport.htm

Motherless Daughters
www.dfwnet.com/md

Rainbows
www.rainbows.org or 1-800-266-3206
This is an organization that through its curricula "provides bridges to emotional healing for children, adolescents, and adults confronting death, divorce, and other painful family transitions."

Reviews

At Crescent Elementary School in Waldwick, New Jersey, during the 1998 to 1999 school year we adopted and implemented *Rainbows* (Marta and Laz) as a program for students who are grieving. The mission of *Rainbows* is to provide bridges to emotional healing for children, adolescents and adults confronting death, divorce and other painful family transitions. This was accomplished by having Rainbows staff conduct training for the volunteers who led the small groups over a sixteen-week period. The curriculum, activities, workbooks and directions were excellent. The experience for faculty, parents and students who were involved was reported by all as "healing and helpful." Plans to repeat the program in the coming years is underway. For further information, call Crescent School at 201-445-0690.

To read or contribute a review of any programs or materials such as the one above, visit the Web site at *www.kidsgrieve.org*.

Section D:
Additional Information

Definitions of Emotional Responses

Anger—powerful response to fear, hurt, threat, harm, and loss that is like a tightly wound spring inside that uncoils instantaneously. The two most common expressions are a suppression that turns the anger inward, back on ourselves, or an expulsion that spews it outward, often on others.

It is very difficult for any of us to imagine being angry with a person who died. And yet this emotional response is one of the most normal and commonly experienced. But because it is so unimaginable there is a tendency to repress and suppress it. But anger at the abandonment and the attendant helplessness is critical for us to acknowledge and confront.

Frustration—a repeating sense of impotence, the inability to change a disappointing or negative circumstance. This often comes in spurts like anger and is similarly suppressed or expressed.

Fear—anticipation of hurt or destruction.

Regret—a longing to undo or redo something in the past.

Longing—a persistent ache for something we have been denied or lost.

Guilt—words or actions for which we feel responsible and wish we could change.

Loneliness—a sense of being alone, even with others around us.

Hurt—a pain of heart or mind or body or soul.

Resentment—a negative feeling toward others who have what we have been denied. Anger that has been held in too long.

Discouragement—the impulse to give up or quit. A loss of courage.

Section D:
Additional Information

Self-Pity—feeling sorry for ourselves. Self-defeating thoughts expressed in whining, complaining, moping and other lethargic behavior.

Sadness—the opposite of happiness, which depends on "happenings." Sadness is the normal feeling associated with a negative "happening."

Betrayal—when events or people have turned against us, withdrawn their love or presence or support.

Anxiety—a pervasive, nagging sense that something is wrong or will be wrong. Waiting for the "other shoe to drop."

Worry—repetitive thinking about current problems and the potential hurts, failures and impending illnesses that could result from the problems.

Panic—seizures of anxiety and worry that prevent us from functioning.

Despair—the lack of desire to go on working, trying, feeling, caring or living.

Relief—a lifting of oppressive, negative feelings, responsibilities, or obligations.

Confusion—an inability to think clearly or act sensibly.

Self-Absorption—unable to focus on others, their needs or circumstance. All thoughts and actions are self-directed.

Destructive Thinking—the absence of hope or positive expectations. Negative expectations that often become self-fulfilled prophecy.

Destructive Behavior—acting out destructive tendencies, through either conscious or unconscious impulses.

UNDERSTANDING THE ROLE OF EMOTIONS IN GRIEF

The human experience is a complicated interplay of thoughts and feelings. And the question that is on all of our minds is which of these is primary? Do our thoughts direct our feelings or do our feelings direct our thoughts? The answer, of course, is both. Most of us desire that our thoughts, the ideas that are in our minds, have primary power; we want our thoughts to direct how we feel. This being the case, we could always demand that we feel happy, peaceful, productive, upbeat and positive. Most of us actually try to do this, desiring that our feelings obey our will. The danger, of course, is that we become rigid and keep such a tight lid on our feelings and emotions, under the iron fist of our thoughts, that we stifle our emotions. This is not healthy.

The converse, allowing ourselves to be flooded by emotions, having our thoughts constantly overruled by what we feel, and having no control over our feelings, is equally unhealthy. Being at the mercy of out-of-control feelings prevents peaceable living and successful functioning. So, while it is healthy to allow emotions to have expression, it can be injurious to be ruled by them. It is critical to have your feelings come to open expression, and that they inform your thoughts and ideas.

Obviously then most of us try to cope and function by striking a balance between our feelings and our thoughts. And on most days the majority of us do well enough. But in considering the effects of a trauma, a loss, or any upsetting experience in our life, this delicate balance between our thoughts and feelings gets disrupted and we get tossed over.

Our equilibrium is lost. In many ways, this describes the experience of a loss. Our thoughts can no longer control our feelings; our feelings can no longer direct our thoughts. So at its essence, the experience of grief and loss is one where we have lost the balance that we had worked so hard to achieve between what we feel and what we think. Suddenly we find ourselves tipping to one side or the other like a wheelbarrow that is too full. And it is in trying to regain our equilibrium that we try all sorts of strategies to correct what we are thinking and feeling. One moment our thoughts keep our feelings at bay, the next instant our clarity is deluged by a tidal wave of erupting emotions, like overwhelming sadness or anger.

The fact is, when a loss has been suffered, it is critical to recognize that we can never have the same equilibrium. It is lost forever. One effect of a life-changing loss is that we will never feel the exact same way again. We will never think the same way again, in relation to that loss or losses. We need to form a new equilibrium, because we cannot reestablish the old. And it takes time to come to terms with and acknowledge the new thoughts we have and the new feelings we experience.

Emotions don't come out of thin air; we usually have an emotional reaction to a stimulus, in other words, to an event. Something happens and we respond with the emotion of joy or surprise, shock or sadness, terror or longing. Interestingly, then, those same emotions alter over time. We may not always be aware of what the stimulus is; it could be a smell or the weather or a time of year. When there is a sudden death or trauma, shock may mute or blunt emotions completely. This biological surge-protector helps us while we regain our emotional equilibrium. Then over time the feelings of sadness, aching and longing slowly surface, and we begin the process of accommodating those feelings in our lives. There is a high degree of variability in how this happens, depending on the individual person. We have different emotional reactions at different moments and different times in response to grief.

Since emotions are physical and psychological, everyone can tell about times when their feelings felt painful or made them sick. So when we think about teenagers in the middle of growth and hormonal changes the likelihood is great that they will experience their emotions more intensely, with more volatility and more unpredictability. They tend to change from moment to moment, more than they would if they were very young or if they were older, more mature. Some kids are terribly depressed, some kids get angry, some kids are agitated and don't know why. But the biggest factor, perhaps, is the frequency with which they change and the intensity of their change. Conversely, young children don't express their emotion as predominantly, and often we misread them.

I wonder why it is that when people are overcome with emotion that makes us feel uncomfortable, like regret or guilt, a common reaction is irritability. Does one emotion trump another emotion? If we start feeling sad or scared do we use anger to replace the more vulnerable feeling? Are we more comfortable with anger and irritation? Do they make us feel more powerful? The emotions surrounding death bring up the ultimate existential fears of our own demise, leaving us feeling vulnerable and abandoned. So, for a child the stakes are even higher. Not only could it happen to me, they may think, but if it happened to my mother or father, then what would I do?

Another interesting experience for children is the fantastical or magical thinking that goes on, like "I caused this, or if I hadn't done that, none of this would have happened." Remember the little boy who wrote the leaf that said, "My little brother Michael is in heaven. Mrs. Small, maybe you could teach him how to read." That was an expression of his fantasy about what was going on with Mrs. Small and where is heaven and what's it like. I believe this is where art therapy is so helpful. By drawing out a fantasy or fear with an experienced therapist, children begin to understand reality and can find new ways to cope with the changes their new reality brings.

For the schools or parents, it is important to know that childhood or teenage emotions can fool us and can be masks for other deeper emotions. Not everyone has the skill to interpret them, although a caring, loving parent or teacher can do some of the guidance work in disentangling the emotions of their kids. But, it is probably safe to say that surface emotions in our students are most likely masquerading for some fairly fundamental predictable emotions: fear of loss of their caretaker, fear of this happening to them, fear of where their emotions might take them. And that gives parents and teachers a clue about what to do.

Understanding Anger (from *Mourning and Dancing*)

ANGER appears to be the number-one emotion that causes grief (excuse the pun) for grieving people. I grew up thinking that anger was bad, and that good people, especially good church people did not get angry. Well, I certainly have learned a lot about anger that disputes my upbringing. First of all, the church message I learned was not scriptural. The Bible does not say, "Don't be angry." It says, "don't let the sun go down on your anger," and "be slow to anger," and "be angry but sin not." Now, from a mental-health point of view, these are constructive directives. Not letting the sun go down on your anger means work it out so you can sleep. Being slow to anger can be helpful if you are the type that flies off the handle and you need an anger management strategy. And my interpretation of not sinning while angry is to not do anything to hurt yourself or others in the heat of your anger. The important message here is that I do not hear the words "do not be angry," which I believe is impossible.

Our dear friend Dr. Neil Warren has helped me understand ANGER as I had never understood it before. In his book, *Make Anger Your Ally*, he explains that anger is a state of preparedness or physical readiness that emerges when we are threatened, frustrated, rejected or hurt, all of which are experienced when we suffer loss. "Since everyone has a body that automatically prepares for action in the face of life's provoking events, everybody has anger. Anger is the spring that coils in you, an intricately designed internal process which gives you the capacity to manage the difficult and threatening parts of your life." It is an internal part of our natural defense system and is no worse than closing your eyes and turning your head away if something is threatening your face. No one would think ill of you for that. Yet the same gesture when someone is asking you for help or saying "I love you" can have a devastating effect. The same is true of anger, if used hurtfully. So the crucial variable here is what do we do with our anger, this necessary state of preparedness. Do we use it to lash out against others, destroying whatever is in our path, or do we turn it inward against ourselves, denying that it exists, similar to saying the "emperor is wearing no clothes." If turned inward, denied, repressed, it will be just as destructive as outward expressions, except the results too often lead to diminishing health, bodily injury, depression, and sometimes suicide. This latter response is more common with women and is powerfully present throughout the grieving process. A woman in one of my support groups, whose husband had been tragically killed, insisted week after week that she was not angry, until we helped her give it different names. And she began to give voice to her frustration, panic, fear and desire to retaliate. What happened, when she allowed herself, in the safety and understanding of this group, to express feelings, was an emerging ability to understand this natural internal response. And one evening this gentle, soft-spoken, refined, religious woman told us that when she saw couples walking together, hand-in-hand, something would rise up inside of her that felt like boiling water, and, secretly, what she wanted to do was kill them. To which I gently suggested that this might be a pretty good description of anger. She agreed and immediately asked what she could do about it. I suggested that she might find clues to that by talking about what she routinely does with these feelings and by understanding that we tend to handle anger in a similar manner to others in our lives who have been models for us. She bowed her head and said her mother never got angry and had always told her that anger was a sin. Her mother also told her that sometimes men can't help it, but for women, good women, it was not something you do. So, we discussed the powerful messages passed down from generation to generation that become ingrained cultural mores. I explained what

I had learned from Neil Warren about what happens to her when she sees obliviously happy couples and what happens to men and women alike every day. What she learned is that "anger is a powerful force. You can suppress it, deny it, let it control you or learn to manage it. You can make anger work for you, instead of against you." Then I told her the story of my three-year-old Tommy tearing up the photos of the Daddy he loved and missed so deeply. He was too young to have learned unhealthy cultural mores, and his innocent anger was expressed in ripping up the pictures that could not pick him up, hold him tight and ease the ache he didn't begin to understand. This processing, this "anger work" is a large, ongoing part of grief recovery.

Section E:
Writing Through the Storm

Letters and other writings have been reported by many who are grieving as the next best thing to a support group. They can be pulled out of a drawer or up on a desktop at any hour of the day or night. The ones offered here are a sampling of what we can do to help each other over time. The expressions on the faces of individuals who handed me the following testify that words of remembrance and honor stand the test of time. Those who have a hard time speaking what is in their hearts can rest assured that the written word is a lasting gift.

JASON REMEMBERS HIS FRIEND MANDY

"Hey, Whit, before she leaves, let me get a picture." I was sitting in a chair, but even then I was almost the same height as Mandy Jackson. Only around five feet tall and less than a hundred pounds, Mandy was diminutive in stature only. She was larger than life in everything else that she did. Always one to play for an audience, Mandy flung her arms around me and pressed her head close to mine. The flash exploded, and my eyes tingled from the aftermath of the sudden burst of light.

"I'm gonna miss you, Hon," Mandy said, as she placed a gentle kiss on my cheek. She had taken to calling everyone "Hon" lately, but for some reason, I felt special when it was directed toward me. That was what made Mandy so priceless: She always made whomever she was talking to feel like they were special, even though she was always in a hurry. If you wanted to talk, she would focus on you with those piercing eyes. And you knew the words coming out of your mouth were much more important to her than a simple question about the chemistry homework or a comment about the basketball team.

She draped her tiny arms over my broad shoulders for one final bear hug, squeezed my arm and smiled at me with those beautiful eyes. Mandy was great at smiling with her eyes. We were at a going-away party being thrown in my honor. I was leaving to begin my college football career at the University of Illinois the next day, four days after high school graduation, and I was filled with a sense of sadness as I watched my long-time friend leave. For the first time, I knew that the glory days of high school were finally over. I did not know that was the last time I would hear Mandy's cheerful voice, hug her miniature frame or be gazed upon by those smiling eyes. I did not know that was the last time I would see my friend.

For two brief weeks during the seventh grade, Mandy and I tried to elevate our relationship to boyfriend-girlfriend. During that time, I was first allowed to see a vulnerable side of Mandy that she usually kept to herself. I always walked her to the bus after school. One day as we walked, we were talking about a big basketball game that she had that night. She was so nervous! As her anxiety mounted, she slipped her tiny hand into mine, and my stomach tightened like it usually does before kickoff on Saturday afternoons. While she waited for her bus, she pulled down slightly on my hand and craned her neck skyward. I bent over and our lips met somewhere in the middle.

As we got older, Mandy's circle of friends got wider and wider. To those who were close to her, Mandy proved an invaluable friend. During high school, Mandy and I remained close. We never tried to date again. The first kiss became the last. We both had relationships outside our friendship. There was never any anger, never any jealousy. There was nothing but a deep love and caring for the welfare of one another. Countless times when I faced a sticky situation, usually involving a girl, I asked her for advice. She was always a clear thinker, and she told me what she thought, even if it was not necessarily what I wanted to hear. We had an honest and trusting friendship that was too strong to be risked by tiptoeing around the truth.

I remember a school dance with Mandy. It was the spring of our senior year and we already could feel the pull of our impending freedom. The student council was hosting a welcome dance for the incoming freshman, the current eighth-graders, and as council members, we were required to attend. It was always entertaining to watch the eighth-graders from each of the middle schools unite for the first time as the next class of Harrison High School. The young-sters were so worried about seeming cool. Three big groups, one from each of the middle schools, would form in oppo-site areas of the cafeteria as the deejay pumped out song after song. It was considered uncool to mix with people you did not know.

Our job, as veterans of the high school scene, was to force the kids to mingle. Mandy was brilliant. She mingled. She mixed. She grooved. She cast her spell on dozens of starstruck eighth-graders. She opened their eyes and gave them an example of what it meant to be really cool. Then she drew me into the mix. I was the exact opposite of Mandy: big and awkward, uncomfortable making a spectacle of myself. And I can't dance. But Mandy decided that on this night I was going to learn. I couldn't say no.

So that night, in front of hundreds of eighth-graders, I learned how to dance, or at least I tried. Mandy got my arms flapping and my legs moving as fast as I could pick

them up. I am sure that next to Mandy, a show-stopping
dancer, I looked like a large ape getting agitated when visitors throw peanuts at it in the zoo. As I plodded through my
lessons with slow feet and stiff hips, mumbling "I feel stu-
pid" about every ten seconds, Mandy only laughed and
encouraged.

"I'll bet all these little eighth-graders are afraid they're
going to become seniors and act like us," she said. She was
probably right. But if some of them turn out to be half the
person Mandy was, I wish they would call me, because I'll
take all the friends like her I can find.

On my first Friday at Illinois, four days into my new life,
the phone rang just as I arrived home from work. It was my
Dad. Mandy Jackson had been killed, he said. She had
been waiting at a railroad crossing behind two other cars,
but she could see that the train was still a good distance
away. Mandy, as usual, was in a hurry. No barricades
blocked the tracks, only flashing lights. Mandy pulled out
from the line of cars and sped towards the intersection. She
actually beat the train that she saw. A second train, however, coming from the opposite direction had been hidden
from her view. It hit the side of her Chevy Cavalier head-on.
Her car was sandwiched between the two locomotives,
shredding the car and instantly robbing my dear friend of
her life.

I kept a letter that Mandy gave me at my going-away
party next to the picture taken that same night. In the snapshot, Mandy has her arms around my neck, and her eyes are
smiling. The letter is one of my most personal possessions.
It is her handwriting, written with a pen that she used, on
paper that she held. When I read it, my friend is, for a brief
instant, brought back to life, and I am no longer alone. I can

hear her voice reading the words and I am tricked for a moment into thinking that she is back home, waiting to hear from me, as she said she would be. The words that Mandy wrote to me on the eve of my departure are the words that I wish I had told her: "I'm just starting to realize how much I'll miss you! You have helped me look into myself and figure out the person I would like to be."

By Jason Wilson

CORY REMEMBERS HIS FRIEND JOBY

The date was May 18, 1997. I should know; it was my birthday. Some of my friends decided to get together at a friend's house. Sean and Joby were a couple of buddies that came over that day. It was around 11:00 A.M. when I got to Ambyr's house. Up the road I noticed a huge truck, kind of like a one-ton truck or dump truck. Since Ambyr's grandparents are farmers, I thought it might be one of her grandpa's trucks. When I got closer and closer, I noticed that the truck magically had changed into an ambulance. I wondered what was going on. Despair and worries went through my head. When I pulled into the drive, I noticed that Sean was sprinkled with blood. His hands were on top of his forehead, and he kept repeating, "Oh my God, what have I done?" Ambyr, Tab and Alina were crying, and they tried to explain what happened. Joby was on the ground, still, motionless, almost as if there was no more soul in his body to let him move with ease. His hands and face already were black, blue and purple. It was kind of like a movie, but happening in real life. As Tab told me the story, I could imagine the movement of Joby's feet and hands when he got into the accident.

The story was that Sean and Joby got out the four-wheeler and electric golf cart. They played around awhile and Joby decided to put the golf cart away and called for Sean to come in, too. Sean said that Joby headed toward him in second gear like he was playing chicken. Sean was over by the road heading toward the house, so he began acting like he was playing chicken with Joby. Sean got close enough so that Joby bolted to the right, just as Sean bolted to the left, causing the collision. Joby did a flip in the air and hit the ground head first, causing his neck to snap. Sean got a black eye from Joby as he went through the air. The doctor said that Joby died instantly.

After school the next day we had a get-together at a friend's house to talk about Joby and pray for him. It was a beautiful day; you couldn't have asked for it to be more beautiful. When I pulled down the street tons of cars were already there. Everybody was in the backyard. When I opened the gate, everybody stared at me. I felt like I was in the "Twilight Zone." In a matter of seconds, they started to sing happy birthday to me. That brought a smile to my face.

In the house, the preacher started a prayer and wanted everybody to talk. A Christian boy named Luke, one of my best buds, started to say some words. I can't remember any of the words he said, because in my mind I was remembering the scene I saw with Joby. How I wish I could have helped him, but there was nothing I could have done. I had to just sit there and stare at the paramedics working on him. Boy, did that make me sick, so sick it brought a tear to my face, then another and another. Remembering the good old times that he and I used to have. After people started to see me cry they said that they couldn't hold back any longer. Emotional tears went through everybody that day.

The next day was the funeral and six of us friends were pallbearers. We were all best buddies with Joby. Since the funeral was in the high school auditorium, there were no classes that day. All of us were dressed in our best suits. The auditorium was packed, and there weren't enough seats for everyone. I had to get up in front of everyone and give a speech in front of the whole town. I was so nervous that I didn't get to sleep until 3:00 A.M. the night before. I still hadn't written my speech when the funeral started. I figured my friends would help me out. I used the back of the pamphlet they gave out at the funeral and tried to write it in fifteen minutes. A funeral is not the most comfortable place to write a speech. I would write and erase, write and erase.

My palms were sweating when I took the podium. I was thinking, *Why am I up here?* The spotlight blinded me, and I couldn't see anybody. But I could feel their eyes on me like knives cutting me down to size. Somehow, the words flew out of my mouth like a bird in the morning sun. "Hello, my name is Cory Malchow and I have a story to tell about Joby and Sean, who were best friends. An hour before the accident, Joby and Sean were talking about the things they wanted to do before they died. They both agreed that they wanted to go skydiving. Since Joby can't jump out of an airplane, today I promise to go skydiving for him."

By Cory Malchow

MANDY REMEMBERS HER FRIEND AMITY

(Amity died earlier in the same school year, before Mandy)

As I stood at the gym door I became dizzy with emotion.
From looking at all the other faces in the room, I could tell
I wasn't the only one feeling this way. A long line of people
stretched from the entrance of the school all the way to the
coffin. All around people were crying. They clutched their
tissues and tried to mop up the small rivers flowing from
their eyes.

The scenery, despite the atmosphere, was beautiful. The
bright flowers carpeted the floor like a meadow. Each color
tried to grab our attention and offer some warmth and comfort. Their sweet smell was as relaxing as a nap in the sun.
Slowly I approached the coffin. The dark wood shined and
reflected the gym lights. An arrangement of flowers lay deli-
cately across the closed half of the coffin. Inside lay a beautiful young lady. Her gently raised eyebrows and slightly
upturned lips made it appear as though she was enjoying
her eternal rest. To the touch, her skin felt like ice. She
reminded me of a mannequin, so still and pale yet artisti-
cally designed with makeup to look as though life existed
inside her. At the end of the coffin was a showcase of pictures. I looked at a photo from her childhood and couldn't
help but smile. The thick spectacles on her nose were two
huge magnifying glasses connected by a band of plastic. Her
curly brown hair laid in a frizzy mess on her head. A big
goofy smile added to her funny appearance. I moved on,
examining another photo taken many years later. Long
locks of dark hair skimmed lightly over her high cheek-
bones, accenting the brightness in her eyes. The now tall
and slender body demanded attention from anyone around

her. Her transformation from an awkward child into a graceful young lady was much like the metamorphosis of a caterpillar into a butterfly.

I walked out of the gym feeling a sense of peace. The air seemed lighter and easier to breathe. I understood that she had gone on to a better place to live, and for a brief moment I was actually happy. Knowing that she had lived her life to the fullest gave me hope that I might do the same with mine. I felt privileged for having known this special person whose memory would always remain in my heart.

By Amanda Jackson

Part V

Full Circle

A s I think about the Circle of Life and our journeys of grief, I have come to value the moments when we experience coming "full circle." When my son, Tom, played football in high school on his father's field, a beloved, retired coach took him aside to tell him what a great guy his father was. Tom listened with respect and then said, "Yes, Sir, I know. My mother has told me all about him." In that moment, I felt something come full circle. When our daughter, Tamara, became the president of an Internet company, I watched her direct her team with the same depth of commitment and zeal her Dad used when he was coaching, and something came full circle. When I held in my hands the newly published book that tells all of our stories, again, I felt the same sense of completion and it happened again just this week, when a woman came up to me after a support group meeting and said, "I had to come back in here and tell you something. I feel better. This has helped. I think I am going to make it."

Coming full circle is a sweet thing, whenever it comes, and I am finding myself in the middle of such an experience as I finish this book for you. As this academic year ends in

Carolyn Small's school, we are preparing the dedication of her memorial garden and this book is dedicated in her memory.

Now there is a new circle beginning its course, this valuable work of helping our students, our children, as they go through life's losses and grieve. The essence of this vision or philosophy was captured in a speech I gave in New Jersey, to the Ramapo Valley Administrators Association, of which Carolyn and I both were members. In this speech, I gave these administrators an overview of healthy grief work through my own story and the story of Carolyn Small's school. I gave them a glimpse into what this work looks like in the classroom, and I told them how a team could work in their schools. I also tried to honor their colleague who had died. I offer it now as a fitting conclusion to this book and a tribute to all of my colleagues across the country who will dare to join this circle.

Ramapo Valley Luncheon

It is my pleasure to be here in New Jersey with you today. I have had lunch in this room many times with Ramapo Valley Administrators, and some of your faces are familiar and some of your faces are new. The first time I came here was in 1986, and I never dreamed I'd be standing before you this year in a whole other field of work. But, here I am, and I have to tell you I love doing what I am doing.

When I was twenty-four years old, I had not finished college. I had married my high school sweetheart, who had a full football scholarship and we went to school together. While we were there, we had a couple of babies and I was only taking one course a semester. The year that Bob graduated, and became a teacher and coach in a high school in the Midwest, he contracted a rare form of cancer, and died nine days after it was diagnosed. Now, I had these two babies, and no degree and no marketable skills, unless you counted detasseling corn in Indiana a marketable skill. I really did not know what to do. I was desperate; I was heartbroken. And so in my youth and ignorance and heartache, I ran away. I was at least smart enough to run back to school and get my teaching degree. And then I took my two little preschoolers and moved to New Hampshire. There in the White Mountains we began an odyssey through the East Coast that eventually brought me to Bergen County and to Waldwick, where Joe Maas hired me as a school principal. I gained a number of degrees along the way, not only to advance my career but also in an attempt to make myself feel that I was credible. One of the things that grief does to you is make you feel like there is something wrong with you. I had only a couple of models to follow, Jackie Kennedy and Coretta Scott King, both of whom looked like they had it together, and I sure didn't feel like I did. They heard the messages from our society loud and clear: "pull yourself up by your bootstraps," "put on a happy face," "smile though your heart is aching," "you need to get over it and get on with your life." Well, I don't think that strategy works. It didn't work for me. When our grief would come up, as a profound loss in your life will come up many times over a lifetime, what was I to say to two little children, "Are you over losing your father?" That's like saying to somebody's whose legs have been cut off, "Are you over that now?" I mean, I like to talk about the fact that loss over time comes up from time to time, but it's not with you all the time. And that doesn't mean you can't be happy. What seems to be a problem for people, especially children, is when no one allows them to acknowledge their loss. No one allows them to acknowledge their pain. And that is where our society still is today. Look at all the recent tragedies that we have seen in the media. Starting with Columbine High School, I mean, the message is, "get over it." The question everyone wants answered is "how long does it take to get over it?" You can't imagine how many times people say, "Sally, what do you think, how long will it take?" Not only does everyone want us to get over it, but we are also supposed to find closure. I hate this word "closure." I've said in my book that I don't think there's room for the word "closure" in grief work. Closure is something you do with a door. What does closure mean anyway? That you separate yourself away from your loss, you have no feelings about it, that you have no memories about it, that there is no pain connected to it? Well, those are unrealistic expectations. When my daughter, who was four when her father died, was twenty-six, she was married. So, now picture me at her wedding. I'm sitting in a pew, I hear the wedding march, I look up the aisle and there is our daughter, the most beautiful bride in the world. Was I "over it"? Did I "forget" that her father should be there? Did I not feel the injustice that her father wasn't there for any of the big events in her life, other than her birth? No! So why do we expect that? Why would we as a nation forget how to remember? Other cultures do it. I think the Jewish faith does it well. But we who make up the majority of our modern culture are becoming forgetful in this area. We've forgotten how to remember; we've forgotten how to honor. Our veterans do it well. But, personally we don't give each other time or space or direction or encouragement to remember and grieve and honor those we have lost.

Our colleague Carolyn Small was a whirlwind. I said at her funeral that in honor of her life and her service the Waldwick Board of Education had closed all of the schools for the day. And I said the last time they did that was for Hurricane Floyd and on that day they closed them for a whirlwind named Carolyn Small. She was a dynamo. She had a sweater for every holiday and every season and every activity that existed. She was a progressive educator with a vision, who rallied many to the cause and drove other people absolutely crazy. Because she wanted it all today, she wanted it all right now and she wanted everybody on the same page. Well, we are administrators and we know that the staff is seldom moved in that kind of unanimous manner and on the same timetable, but she made great strides. She left an imprint on this school that I knew nothing about and I was the principal of the school on the other side of town last year. We became great friends. You know how that happens when we work together in the trenches. She came to visit me in August, and she kept saying, "I don't believe you live in Indiana, why would anyone want to live in Indiana? There's no good Italian food in Indiana!" I said, "You know, you just need to come and see for yourself." So, the week before school started she came to Indiana. We took pictures of her on a John Deere tractor, we took her out into a cornfield, we gave her the full Midwestern experience. We took her to our very best restaurants, all of which you know didn't measure up. Every day she would get up and say she was going to help me write, because I had a deadline of October 30 for my next book, *Mourning and Dancing for Schools: A Grief and Recovery Sourcebook for Students, Teachers and Parents.*

Now ask me if I met that deadline. No, because she died October 9 and I have been here running her school, helping them grieve. Isn't it ironic that I've been in her school and in a way she's helping me write my book. I can almost hear her saying, "See, I told you I would help you." That was Carolyn's style.

When I came to her school, our crisis management team, under the direction of Jack Szabo and Carol Lynch, did one of the best jobs I've ever seen, and for fifteen years I have been doing this work in schools when tragedies occur. They had excellent materials prepared for the staff that were age-appropriate for the children in their charge. They had letters for parents, they had information for teachers, they had ways for teachers to talk to kids, they had counselors in every classroom, in every building. I think schools across the country do this well. Maybe there are some exceptions, but for the most part we in the public schools have learned to do crisis management well. We get the information out, we hold ceremonies, we make plaques, and we dedicate pages in a yearbook, we name things in honor of these kids or teachers, and we determine funds and memorial scholarships. I think we do this well. But, here's my question: What are we doing for the kids to process their grief a week later, when all the flowers are dead and all the food has gone bad and needs to be cleaned out of the refrigerator? What do we do a month later? What do we do six months later, a year later? Because you and I know that's when it comes up. This crisis stuff is shock. And shock is like the surge protector that we have on our computers that keeps it from short-circuiting when struck by lightning. Shock is just like that. Those of you that have been there, and most of you have at one time or another, know that you feel like you're in a bubble, amazed that you go through the motions of life. People talk to you and you answer but you can't remember where you were, you can't keep track of things. If there's anything I learned during the shock of that first week after Carolyn's death it's that I can't do this grief work when I'm grieving. This is the first time I've done it and I won't ever do it again, because I was struggling. I struggled while we were talking to the teachers an hour and a half before school started. Then we brought in the kids and I struggled through the time with them and then with the parents. What happens when you're in shock is you can put out a little bit, and then all of a sudden you kind of shut down, you just kind of stand and stare. That's what happened when I was talking to parents and giving them ideas about how to talk to their children and what's important about crying and laughing and all of those things. When a parent asked me a question, I said, "I beg your pardon." And she asked again, but she might as well have been speaking another language. I said, "Well, uh . . . let's see," and I just ignored her. Then I started to say something else and one of our school social workers said, "Oh, Sally, one way we could answer that mother's question is. . . ." And I realized what was happening. I, too, was in shock. I was grieving; this was my friend and my colleague, and my system "zoned out." I had been "giving out" since seven o'clock this morning and then I had nothing more to give. I just shut down. Then I decided that this was important information to give to teachers, to the parents. There's just so much you can do, so pace yourselves. I told them that no one was allowed to say, "Pull yourself up by your bootstraps." I told them that

I was a good example of how it works, and it's very helpful to just acknowledge what's real.

Later when I regained some strength, I spent a lot of time going into the classrooms, talking with kids. Fifth-grade boys, of course, wanted to know details about how it happened. How did the car roll over? Did she have on her seat belt? You know what, that's important information. We need to tell the story and we need to tell it as honestly and simply as we can. And when those boys felt like someone was being honest with them, they were okay. By letting them ask questions and retell the story we can reduce any magical thinking or any fantastical thinking. You know kids get into their fantasies and imagine how things might have been, what went wrong, and what might happen to them or, even worse, their parents. Leaving students alone without adult guidance can lead to what happened in Bergenfield. There were a couple of student deaths and then shocking copycat suicides that took place in the aftermath. That is clear indication that something is going on in kids' brains where we adults are not reaching, that we need to normalize, that we need to neutralize, that we need to acknowledge and address.

Now, how are we going to do this? We can't hire any new staff, we don't have any money, how are we going to do that? Well, what I am suggesting is that we train a team. This team can be made up mostly of teachers, teachers who want to be on a loss and grief team, teachers who want to be available. And the reason their presence is important is because they are "there" and they are trusted and they know how the kids they work with tick. When a kid comes into your classroom at the end of the day and says, "I failed everything; my parents are going to kill me; I want to run away," teachers have trained ears to hear what is just below the surface. And that could be something like, "My parents are going through a divorce and my whole life is falling apart." Despondency and irritability and feelings of desperation in kids usually are a thin mask over something that they have lost and are grieving. And if we have a group of people in every school, in every district, we can address that over time, when it comes up. As you know, we have our school psychologists, we have our social workers. They're great at what they do but they can't see all the kids all the time. Now, we need a group that is committed to be trained, to talk about grief and loss, to understand and hear what is normal about grieving, to be able to work with kids and acknowledge their grief, and do more than give them quick, easy steps to get over it. These interventions can dispel some of the long-term effects that our management teams, school psychologists and social workers don't have time to address. You know their schedules; their calendars are full.

The team training will be outlined in my book and available on the Internet at *www.kidsgrieve.org*. Anyone can serve and anyone can do the training. Basically, it begins with members of the team working on dealing with their own losses. Then we talk about grief in general and its emotional, psychological, physical and spiritual effects. For instance, the team will look at issues like why we cry and that physically and emotionally it's good to cry. Crying releases endorphins from the brain that create a sense of well-being and stimulates your immune system. Well, if you're grieving, those are two really good things. Everybody wants to feel better; everybody needs help with their health. So the team needs to understand that we live in a society that says don't do that, don't cry, you need to feel better. To which the reply can be, "but I feel badly right now." Is there something wrong with feeling badly right now? If great grief is a result of great love or great respect, why wouldn't we feel it, why wouldn't we acknowledge it?

The grief and loss team can work together to help each other find ways to talk to kids and learn effective ways to elicit responses. Obviously, something other than, "How are you feeling?" Together they can find phrases, building an arsenal of interactive behaviors and words. We also need to teach this team the red flags that indicate when we call in the school psychologist or social worker and say, there needs to be an intervention here. This is a lay team, we're not doing therapy here, we're just helping kids acknowledge where they are and what's happening in their lives and finding a way to change or incorporate these changes in their lives. If a student has lost a parent or a good friend, or their family has broken up, or they have moved for the fourteenth time since they started first grade, somebody needs to talk to them about what happens in your life when you experience loss. This team can start support groups, they can have evenings where people can dialog about loss, they can start student teams that could become trained. And this can all evolve out of that wonderful pool of people that want to do it, simply because they want to do it. I have not been to a high school yet where I have not had a good turnout. I've seen the team of ten or twelve people come out of that initial session, because people who work in schools with kids see the slow decline that takes place in kids that are grieving. They have watched these kids slip in their work, drop out of extracurricular activities and start to hang out with the wrong people. And everyone knows the frustration of seeing kids go down and feeling like there's nothing we can do. Now, individually there's little we can do. I'm the only crazy person I know that individually goes into a school trying to make a difference. I am at least smart enough to know that the next book that I had to write would be a book about creating teams to do this work. We're not talking about needing any kind of a counseling degree in order to do this work. We already do this in other areas without specialized degrees. We have become very savvy about drug and alcohol abuse, about smoking. We have become comfortable, or as comfortable as we can get, speaking about communicable diseases. So, if we have become comfortable talking about these very difficult, sensitive and even controversial subjects in the public schools, why not break ground in this new frontier? Every time I go and speak someplace I say, "Tell me I'm wrong, tell me you have people in your school who are doing this ongoing grief work. Tell me that you have a group helping kids who are grieving and that their work is advertised and supported. Tell me that there is a group in your school that anybody can go to at any time." I haven't found one yet.

I wish I had been at Columbine High School. Actually, my first book came out in May, and my publisher and I talked about sending me out there. But I said, "I'll be happy to go to Columbine High School, but I want to go next year." I sure wasn't going to go to Columbine High School and bring my new book. This work I'm proposing takes place after the media is gone. This takes place after the crisis management team and all the other counselors have gone back to their regular jobs. This takes place out of the hearts and souls of the people who would want to do this work, who will be excited about doing this work, who will find the time to do it, and who will probably buy the book out of their own pockets. I'm making the worksheets available as templates on *www.kidsgrieve.org*, so people can download them and put their own school names on them. I also want eventually to put the models on the Internet showing how to start a team in church or a team in a Y, because the teams need to be made up of the people who are there. As you and I know, the time that problems come up for kids at school are on the bus, on the way back from the game, after school, on the playground, in the hall or following a class. And it is in that moment or shortly thereafter that we need to have a two- or three-minute intervention in which we can say, "If you need to talk more about this, write down some things and come back to me." All of these strategies are part of the team.

So, that's what I'm doing. I have read at Carolyn's school *The Fall of Freddie the Leaf* to almost every class. It's a beautiful metaphor for life and death and why we're here and how life goes on. It's a book about hope as well as death and grief. I've used some other books—one is *There's No Such Thing as a Dragon*, by Jack Kent. And this is a wonderful example of what my philosophy is. In this book a little boy gets up one morning to find a dragon perched on the footboard of his bed. So he goes downstairs and tells his mother, "There's a dragon in my bed." And, of course, his mother says to him, "You know there's no such thing as a dragon, go upstairs and get dressed for school." And he does, but he notices the dragon is a little bigger when he gets upstairs. And at school he tells his teacher, "You're not going to believe this but in my house, perched on my bed is a dragon." And of course the teacher says, "There's no such thing as a dragon." And the book is a whole series of him going to everybody in his life and telling them the same thing and getting the same response. And every time this happens, the dragon grows.

And it's not until the dragon's head is out the front door, tail out the back, feet out the windows, that the postal carrier comes by and says to the father, "Quite some dragon you have there." And the father says, "Yeah, you're right, it's pretty big." And what happens? The dragon begins to shrink. I think that's the simple description of this work that I'm proposing that we do for kids in school. It's about trying to prevent their dragons from growing and helping them find a way to incorporate loss and grief and change in their lives, so it diminishes over time.

Remembering is a big part of that work. We have remembered Carolyn Small in all kinds of beautiful artwork and letters. We have a tree in the All-Purpose Room in her memory. Every leaf has a message written on it by a student who didn't get a chance to say good-bye or thank you. We have planted bulbs. All of the students in the school had a spade and a bulb in their hands during this past week as we began to build memorial gardens, which will bloom in the spring and will remind them of all that she gave there. I talked with kids in the classroom about what they liked, what they learned, what was good, what did they remember? We listed all those things on the board, and then I said to them, "Can you do these things?" "Can you help kids solve problems, can you have a warm, welcoming smile, can you teach little kids how to be honest, or cooperative, or responsible?" To which they, of course, said, "Yes." And then I reminded them of what Christa McAuliffe said, "If you teach, you touch the future." And I believe, knowing as I do, after twenty-five years of working with people who have died or who are dying, that their greatest fear is that they will be forgotten. There's no reason to forget. Remembering can be one of the sweetest gifts that we give to each other. I am married today. Will Miller is my husband, and I love him dearly. But still, Bob Downham has a special place in my heart where nobody else lives. And there's no reason to not remember all that I have, and all that his children have, and all that his students have, as a result of his presence in our lives. At Carolyn's funeral, I read a small excerpt from the end of my book that says exactly that, and I would like to read from it in closing now. I call it "Heart Mansions."

I find it helpful to think of my heart as a mansion with many rooms. And I can give each person I love his or her own place there. That place belongs to that person and to no one else. Some rooms are larger than others, some more special than others, each is unique. I used to think that you only have a certain amount of love to pass around to all the people in your life. Facing death changed that. Today I believe that the human heart and our capacity to love is unending if we dare to care that much. And it's even almost as though we have a furnace that fuels our mansion with as much love as we are willing to give and share.

What implications does this have to those of us who have suffered loss? What do we do with that room or space in our hearts that we can so clearly identify as empty, as aching, as hurting, so much that it must be broken? Do we put someone or something else in that place? Do we continually go there and pretend that the past is the present? Do we shut the door and pretend nothing ever happened there? Or do we open the door and cry into the darkness, forgetting there are other places and people in our lives? It helped me to extend my metaphor by thinking of these rooms as rooms in a museum, rooms that hold precious and rare artifacts that symbolize love and life that once existed. There are rooms into which I can go and remember, and laugh, and cry. But they are not rooms in which we can stay. People don't live in museums, they only go there to ponder and reflect, and retouch the memory of what once was.

Will I ever put someone else in Bob Downham's space in my heart, or my mother's, or Carolyn Small's, or any of the rooms that belong to people I love or have loved today? No, never. My husband Will has his own room, as does my step-mother, Maggi. Their rooms belong to them and to no one else. But when I want to remember, or when a thought, or a sound, or a twilight, or a fragrance comes, I can slip quietly away to that special place in my heart and whisper with all the love our memories allow, "I'm so glad you were here. Sleep well, good night."

About the Author

Dr. Sally Downham Miller has worked with schools as a speaker, consultant and support group leader in the area of grief and loss for fifteen years. She has led workshops and seminars across the country and is the Executive Director of Mourning and Dancing, Inc., a nonprofit grief recovery organization, in Lafayette, Indiana. She earned her Ph.D. at Purdue University, and has been a teacher, consultant, school administrator and university professor. She and her husband, Dr. Will Miller, live in New York City and West Lafayette, Indiana. You can receive information about her work and her writing and speaking schedule at her Web site: *www.mourninganddancing.com*.

Also from
Sally Downham Miller

Robert Downham died on
Wednesday, August 23, 1967 of
reticulum cell sarcoma. Three
weeks before he died, he did not
know he was sick. Nine days after
diagnosis, he was dead.

Code #6714
Quality Paperback • $10.95

This is his young wife's story, that of his two young
children and all the others whose lives he touched—it is
the story of those who had to keep on living.